CONCEPTS IN ENVIRONMENT

CONCEPTS IN ENVIRONMENT

Edited by

Prof. P.R. TRIVEDI

Chairman

Indian Institute of Ecology and Environment

New Delhi - 110 030

&

Prof. GURDEEP RAJ

Hony. Professor in Environment Science in

I.I.E.E., New Delhi

Reader in Chemistry

D.S. College, University of Delhi,

New Delhi - 110 003

AKASHDEEP PUBLISHING HOUSE

NEW DELHI - 110 002 (INDIA)

AKASHDEEP PUBLISHING HOUSE
4374/4B, Ansari Road, Daryaganj
New Delhi - 110 002
Ph.: 23261597, 23278000
Visit us at: www.anmolpublications.com

Concepts in Environment

Reprint, 1995, 1997

Reprint, 2005

ISBN 81-7158-230-3

PRINTED IN INDIA

Published by Akashdeep Publishing House, New Delhi - 110 002 and Printed at Mehra Offset Press, Delhi.

Contents

Preface

This book is an outstanding attempt to cover every aspect of environment. The basic aim of this title is to expose the young students to the vital concepts in environment. The study of environment has gained tremendous importance due to the dangerous dimensions of environmental pollution which are largely due to the disruption of the natural ecosystems of the world by the activities of man.

The editing of this book is carried out by young experienced editors who are actively engaged in solving environmental problems at various well known institutes.

During the compilation of this book, editors have freely consulted and used various research journals, standard texts, research workers, teachers and subject experts to all of whom the editors are deeply indebted.

The book will prove to be a much useful reference book for all environmentalists including environmental students, biological students, engineers, doctors, city planners, health technicians and agriculture scientists who are engaged actively in the field of environmental analytical investigations including those which deal mainly with pollution, fishery, ecology, agriculture sanitation and health and hygiene.

One of the editors (A.K.) is highly indebted to his wife Manjula for her patience throughout the editing of this book.

We will highly appreciate all comments from users on omissions or shortcomings.

The Editors

1

Introduction

1.1 Environment

The terms environment and habitat refer to a definable place where an organism lives, including both the physical and biologic features of the place. The word environment comes from the French verb environner, to surround, and means surroundings or something that surrounds. It includes "all the conditions, circumstances, and influences surrounding, and affecting an organism or group of organism".

Environment is taken to mean all those which are physical and chemical, organic and non-organic components of the atmosphere, lithosphere and oceans. Environment is the aggregate of external conditions that influence the life of an individual or population, specifically the life of men; environment ultimately determines the quality and survival of life. Organisms and environment are in constant change. Some changes are very rapid, others take thousand of years. The relationship between and among the physical environment (soil, water, air) and organismal environment (p'ant and animal life) constitutes the study of ecology.

Some workers have used the term micro-environment of designating a functional environment, *i.e.* specfic environment of specific organisms. Literally, this term refers to a small environment. But it has been somewhat a relative term. Therefore, this term is used for the immediate environment of an organism.

1.2 Ecology and Environment

Ecology and ecosystems considers the life habits of over two million different kinds of animals and plants, and it takes into account all manner of influences and interactions among them.

An ecosystem is any spatial or organizational unit which includes living organisms and nonliving substances interacting to produce an exchange of materials between the living and nonliving parts.

An ecosystem includes populations, communities, habitats, and environments, and it specifically refers to the dynamic interaction of all parts of the environment, focusing specially on the exchange of materials between the living and nonliving parts.

Ecosystems comprises of four basic components; abiotic substances, producer organisms, consumer organisms, and decomposer organisms.

Elements which are normally very active in biological processes, like oxygen, may be in an abiotic form readily available for living organisms like free O_2 or CO_2, or they may be in an inaccessible form like silicon dioxide (SiO_2) in quartz, a major component of granite.

The word abiotic means "without life" or "nonliving". *e.g.* water, oxygen, nitrogen, and carbon dioxide, are abiotic when they are physically outside living organisms, like air or water, but once within living organisms they become part of the biotic world.

One of the most important qualities of an ecosystem is the rate of release of nutrients from solids, which regulates the rate of function of the entire system.

Producer Organisms

Producer organisms are bacteria and plants which synthesize organic compounds. They are called as autotrophic or self-productive, in which they take inorganic compounds and manufacture organic materials and living protoplasm from them. All green plants are producer organisms including microscopic algae since they show photosynthesis, and some bacteria are producers, as they may show chemosynthesis or photosynthesis.

Consumer Organisms

Consumer organisms are animals that utilize the organic materials directly or indirectly manufactured by plants. Consumers are unable to produce their own organic compounds for basic nutritive purposes. They are called as heterotrophic, that means different or varied in nutritional source. Primary consumers or herbivores directly consume the organic compounds of plant. Secondary consumers may be omnivores or carnivores which depend partially or entirely on other animals for food. Tertiary and quartenarý consumers may be the second, or third-stage predator, *e.g.* a hawk feeding on a wease that in turn consumed a mouse.

Decomposer Organisms

Decomposer organisms are bacteria and fungi that degrade organic compounds. Their nutrition is called as saprophytic, which is, as sociated with rotten and decaying organic material. In a sense they are the digestive organisms of an ecosystems— they reduce the complex organic molecules of dead plants and animals to simpler organic compounds that can be absorbed by green plants as vital nutrients. They provide the final essential link in the cycle of life. These are essential for the renewal of life, for it decomposers were not active, organic compounds would become locked into complex insoluble molecules which could not be utilized as nutrients by plants.

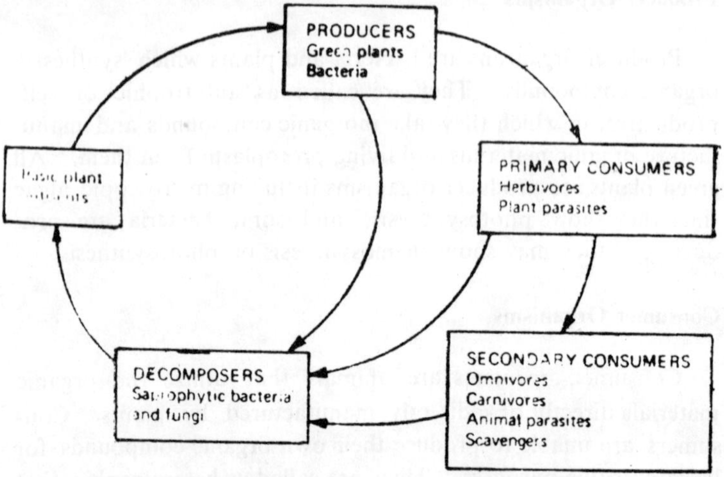

Fig. 1.1. Basic components of an ecosystem

1.3 Environmental Chemistry

In simple words, environmental chemistry may be defined as the study of chemical phenomenon in the environment. A more reasonable definition is "environmental chemistry refers to the study of the sources, reactions, transport, effects and fates of chemical species in the water, soil and air environment".

Environmental chemistry is not a single disciplinary science but a multi-disciplinary science which encompasses many vastly different fields such as chemistry, physics, life sciences, agriculture, medical science, public health, sanitary engineering, etc.

Environmental chemistry is not a new discipline. Excellent work has been done in this field 50 or more years ago. Much of the earlier work was done by non-chemistry groups. In recent years, much of the work on environmental chemistry has been done by chemistry groups.

1.4 Environmental Pollution

For the first time in his entire cultural history, man is facing one of the most horrible ecological crisis – the problem of pollution of his environment which sometime in past was pure, virgin, undisturbed uncontaminated and basically quite hospitable for him.

"Environmental pollution may be defined as the unfavourable alteration of our surroundings, wholly or largely us a by-product of man's actions, through direct or indirect effects of changes in energy patterns, radiation levels, chemical and physical constitution and abundances of organisms. These changes may affect man directly or through his supplies of water and of agricultural and other biological products, his physical objects or possessions, or his opportunities for recreation and appreciation of nature".

The most vital and controversial question left unanswered by this definition of environmental pollution has been the question of what constitutes an "unfavorable alteration". Any man-made alter.tion of the environment probably is having unfavorable effects, at least in the opinion of some people, and favorable effects in the opinion of others, like those whose livelihood depends on an activity that produces pollution. The determination of the extent of the favorable versus unfavorable effects—or of benefits versus costs—has been difficult just because it has been ultimately subjective, even though objective data may get involved in the determination.

The affluent societies of the developed nations of the world have been likely to be more concerned about the unfavorable effects than those nations in which poverty and hunger are major unsolved problems.

Poverty, starvation, and pollution all reflect mankind's failure to design social and political institutions which are capable of properly assessing and controlling technological innovations. Serious problems of poverty and hunger exist in the advanced countries like USA, UK, USSR, etc., despite the progress of the last several decades, and the progress that has been made has been accompained by the aggravation of many existing environmental problems and the production of new ones.

1.5 Evolution of Earth

Before going into the details of the environment we must be funiliar with major changes that have occurred on the Earth.

Although it has been argued that each planet in the solar system has unique features. The dioxygen-rich atmosphere and the presence of life on the Earth is interesting. It was the presence of water rather than oxygen which was crucial to the development of life on Earth, but the present composition of the atmosphere ensures that organisms which can make use of the oxygen in energy-releasing reactions at the Earth's surface are dominant.

The origin of the solar system, including Earth, is controversial because of the various hypotheses are based on our incomplete knowledge of the solar system as it exists now. Further back in time we go the greater the assumptions and extrapolations which are to be made about the conditions that existed then. The evidences indicate that by about 4.5 billion years (4.5×10^9 *a*) ago there was a planet with a solid crust approximately 150 million kilometres from the Sun. Since then major changes have occurred at a much slower rate.

The major structural features of the Earth (Fig. 1.2) are givsn on the next page.

The existing surface of the Earth being irregular, about 70 per cent is covered with water of average depth 4 km (range 0-11 km). The remainder consist of land masses with an average height of 0.84 km (range 0-8.8 km) above sea level. Two-thirds of this land is located in the Northern Hemisphere. The major land masses are called continents and they are defined not by shore-lines but by the edges of the deep-sea platforms, that may be far out to sea; they thus incorporate the continental shelf

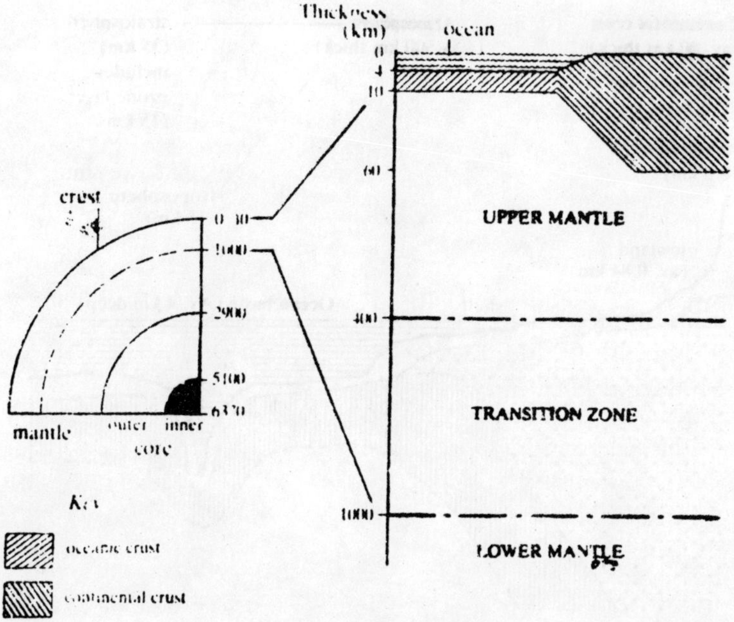

Fig. 1.2. Structure of the Earth

(Fig. 1.3). This definition of continents means that off-shore islands are included as parts of their nearest land masses. Importantly, it agrees with the geological and chemical evidence that there is a compositional difference between continental crustal rocks and the crustal rocks underlying the deep oceans.

Sector	Major elements in order of decreasing concentration
atmosphere	N, O
ocean	O, H (Cl, Na, Mg, S)
sedimentary rocks	O, Si, Al, Fe, Ca, K, Mg, C, Na
granitic igneous rock	O, Si, Al, K, Na, Ca, Fe, Mg
basaltic igneous rock	O, Si, Al, Fe, Ca, Mg
mantle	O, Si, Mg, Fe

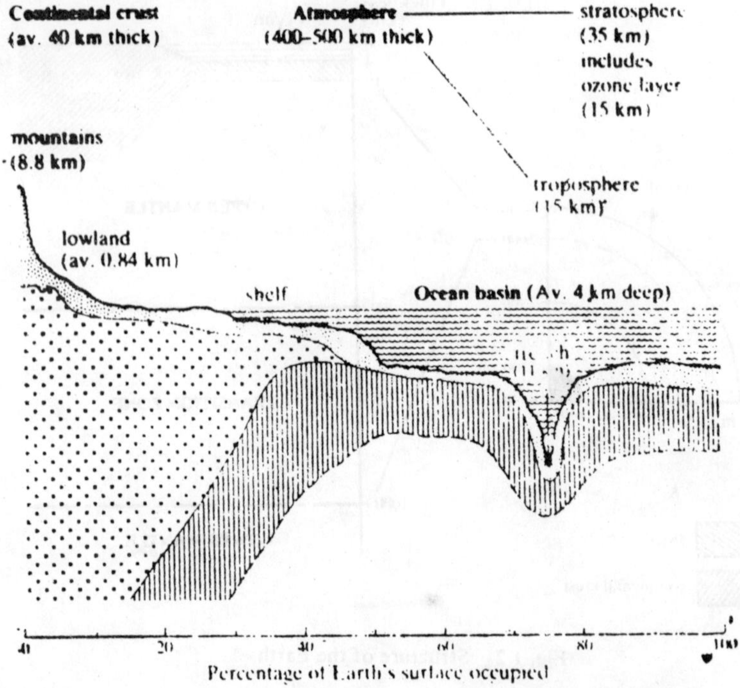

Fig. 1.3. A cross-section of the surface of the Earth indicating the major elements in various sectors

Now it is thought that the surface of the Earth consists of a number of rigid plates (100-150 km thick) moves discontinuously over the mantle (Fig. 1.4). These plates consist of the continental oceanic crusts and the uppermost layer of the mantle. Volcanism is marked by the region, at ocean ridges where two adjoing plates are moving apart by the addition of new crustal material, and by the formation of oceanic basins, *e.g.*, the Atlantic and Indian Oceans. When two plates converge, one plate passes partially under the other to form either an arc-trench system, in oceanic regions, or a mountain belt (*e.g.*, the Himalayas), where two continental regions collide. When crustal material is taken down towards the mantle as one plate rides over the other, the process is termed subduction. This material becomes hotter, and the lower-melting, lighter components may melt and rise towards the surface again, before the denser components mix in with the mantle. The reinjection of these large masses of lighter molten material starts off a mountain-building sequence (Fig. 1.4). Mountain ranges are associated with the convergence of plates.

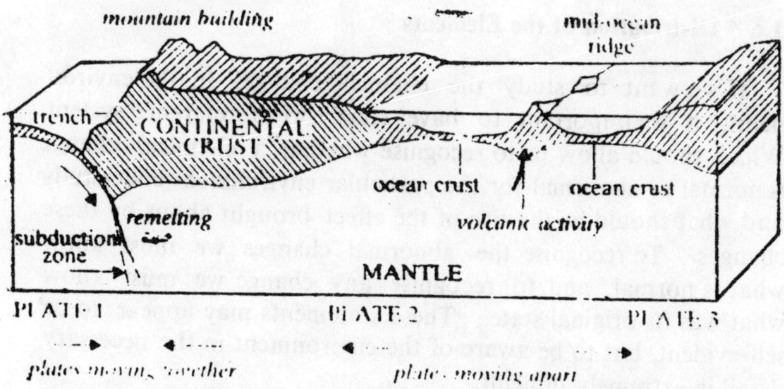

Fig. 1.4. The formation of mid-ocean ridges as plates move apart, and of subduction zones and mountains as plates move together

The relative directions of the movement of adjacent plates changes with time. The plates themselves also change as they break up or merge with adjoining plates, but the overall effect is to keep the irregularity of the Earth's surface contours. An example of change is along the Pacific coast of North America, where two converging plates, the collision of which formed the Rocky Mountain ranges, are now sliding past each other. This lateral movement has produced an extensive transform fault system, the best-known member of that is the San Andreas Fault. The effect of this movement is to separate the Californian coastal region from the mainland and move it northwards towards Canada.

The oldest rocks are 3.8 billion years old. It seems that for at least the past 4 billion years there have been continental areas consisting of less dense (approximately 2.7 g cm^{-3}) rocks rising above the oceanic basins with their more dense (approximately 3.2 g cm^{-3}) rocks. During this length of period the various plates have moved, joined together, broken up and thus caused the formation and destruction of both continents and oceans. Now a days earth-quakes and volcanoes are constant reminders that these large-scale processes are still continuing. However, this book is concerned with processes that occur much more rapidly.

1.6 Distribution of the Elements

If we want to study the chemical changes in the environment, it is important to have some sort of reference system. Which should allow us to recognise whether a chemical change is normal or abnormal for the particular environment understudy and what should be the size of the effect brought about by these changes. To recognise the abnormal changes we must know what is normal, and to recognise any change we must know what was its original state. These statements may appear to be self-evident, but to be aware of the environment in the necessary detail is extremely difficult.

A knowledge of the chemical composition of a system is necessary. Before we can meaningfully study the chemical changes going on in that system. When we come to know about the chemical composition of the various components of our environment (Table 1.1), we realise how many estimates must be included in these figures. It is easy to see tables of numerical values and assume that they are reliable representations of some information. If the information is obtained by chemical analysis, the analysis is said to be 'accurate' if it gives the true value.

Table 1.1

The Ten Major Elements in the Universe, the Earth, the Earth's crust, the ocean, the Atmosphere as Dry Air, and the Biosphere (As Weight %)

Universe	*Earth*	*Crust*	*Ocean*	*Atmosphere*	*Biosphere*
H	Fe	O	O	N	O
77	35	46.6	85.8	75.5	53
He	O	Si	H	O	C

21	29	29.5	11	23.2	39
O	Si	Al	Cl	Ar	H
0.8	14	8.2	1.94	1.3	6.6
C	Mg	Fe	N	C	N
0.3	14	5.0	1.05	9.3×10^{-3}	0.5
Ne	S	Ca	Mg	Ne	Ca
0.2	2.9	3.6	0.13	1.3×10^{-3}	0.4
Fe	Ni	Na	S	Kr	K
0.1	2.4	2.8	0.09	0.45×10^{-3}	0.2
Si	Ca	K	Ca	He	Si
0.07	2.1	2.6	0.041	72×10^{-6}	0.1
N	Al	Mg	K	Xe	P
0.06	1.8	2.1	0.039	40×10^{-6}	0.1
Mg	Na	Ti	Br	H	Mg
0.06	0.3	0.57	0.007	23×10^{-6}	0.1
S	P	H	C	S	S
0.04	0.2	0.22	0.003	70×10^{-9}	0.07

1.7 Geochemical Cycles

From tables such as Table 1.1, it can be seen there of the distribution of the elements, ignore the movement of chemical substances from one of the chosen divisions to another. Rivers are known to carry dissolved and suspended material from the land to the oceans. Movements of plates brings about the uplift of ocean sediments and the formation of new land masses. It is known that plants add dioxygen to the atmosphere by photosynthesis and remove it by respiration. All of these movements might be termed as natural because they had taken place before humans appeared on the Earth. The presence and activities of the human population have brought changes in the rates of movement of many chemical substances and it is the possible effects of these changed rates that have been causing increasing concern. Not only are there increases in transfer rates of compounds already present (such as carbon dioxide, which is being released by the burning of carbon-containing fuels), but completely new chemicals (such as the insecticide DDT) are being distributed on land and sea. The flow of a chemical element between land mass, ocean and atmosphere can be explained by means of a geochemical cycle.

Each geochemical cycle is a model that explains the movement of a chemical element or species, normally near the surface of the Earth. The vast majority of material now near the surface of earth—the crust, the ocean and the atmosphere—stays in this region. Because the movement is both continuous, even if very slow in some cases, and conservative, there is a repeated cycling of the components. The cycles are described using reservoirs, physically well defined units, and transport paths along which material is transferred from one reservoir to another (Fig. 1.5) given on the next page.

The major consequences of the attempts to construct balanced geochemical cycles has been the highlighting of those parts of the cycle about which we know very little.

In quantitative geochemical cycles estimates are made of both the amount of an element in each reservoir and the flux between the reservoirs. The flux can be defined as the amount of material passing along a particular transport pathway in a fixed period of time, generally one year (Fig. 1.5). If the concentration of an element remains constant in a reservoir this means that there is an equilibrium between the amount of element entering the reservoir and the amount leaving. A steady state is reached. Most natural cycles, that is those which are not influenced by human technology, appear on a global basis to be in a steady state. This conclusion has been reached because there is little geological evidence to show that there has been any great change in the global chemical environment over the past few hundred million years.

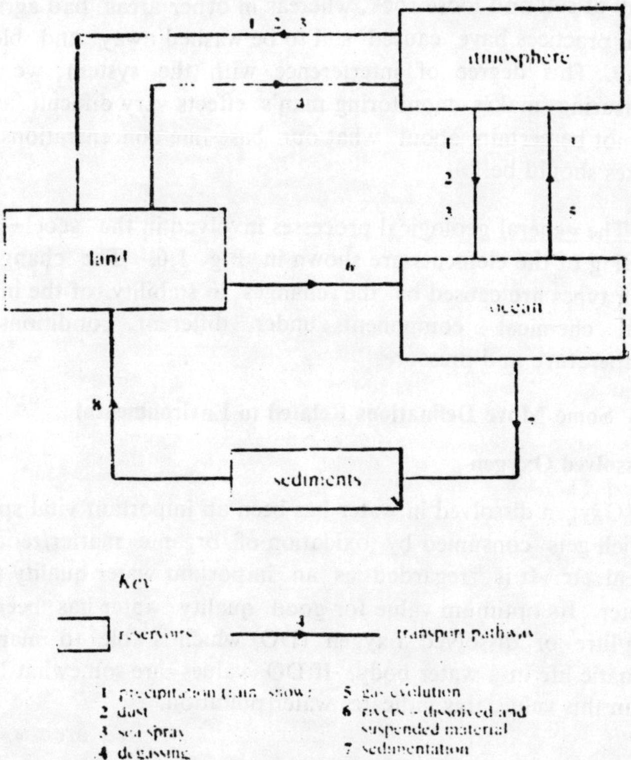

Fig. 1.5. A general model of the geochemical cycle

If it is known that a system is in a steady state, we can evaluate the residence times for individual elements in particular reservoirs (Eqn. 1.1)

$$\text{residence time} = \frac{\text{amount of element in reservoir}}{\text{rate of addition (or removal) of the element}} \quad (1.1)$$

May be the largest impact humans have had on general geochemical cycling processes has been the increase in the rate of transfer of solids from land to sea. This has mainly taken place by disturbing the plants that hold soil in place. In forest areas the cutting down of trees has allowed the rapid washing away of soil and loose rock, whereas in other areas bad agricultural practices have caused soil to be washed away and blown away. This degree of interference with the system we are measuring makes monitoring man's effects very difficult as we cannot be certain about what our base-line concentrations and fluxes should be.

The general geological processes involved in the geochemical cycling of the elements are shown in Fig. 1.6. The changes in rock types are caused by the changes in stability of the individual chemical components under different conditions of temperature and pressure.

1.8 Some Move Definations Related to Environmental

Dissolved Oxygen

Oxygen dissolved in water has been an important vital species which gets consumed by oxidation of organic matter/reducing agent etc. It is regarded as an important water quality parameter. Its optimum value for good quality water has been 4-6 mg/litre of dissolved oxygen (DO) which is able to maintain aquatic life in a water body. If DO values are somewhat lower than this value, this indicates water pollution.

Biochemical Oxygen Demand (BOD)

It is a water quality parameter for organic matter in water, which is empirical in nature. It may be measured by the quantity of oxygen utilised by suitable aquatic microorganisms during a five day period.

Biochemical oxygen demand (BOD) has been a standardized measurement of the amount of oxygen that would be required by microorganisms to cause the decomposition of certain organic and inorganic matter in the water. The measurement is done under standardized conditions (*e.g.*, at 20°C and 5 days to allow the decomposition to take place). The result is called the 5-day BOD and is expressed in milligrams of oxygen per litre of water. BOD is not a pollutant but an indicator. It measures

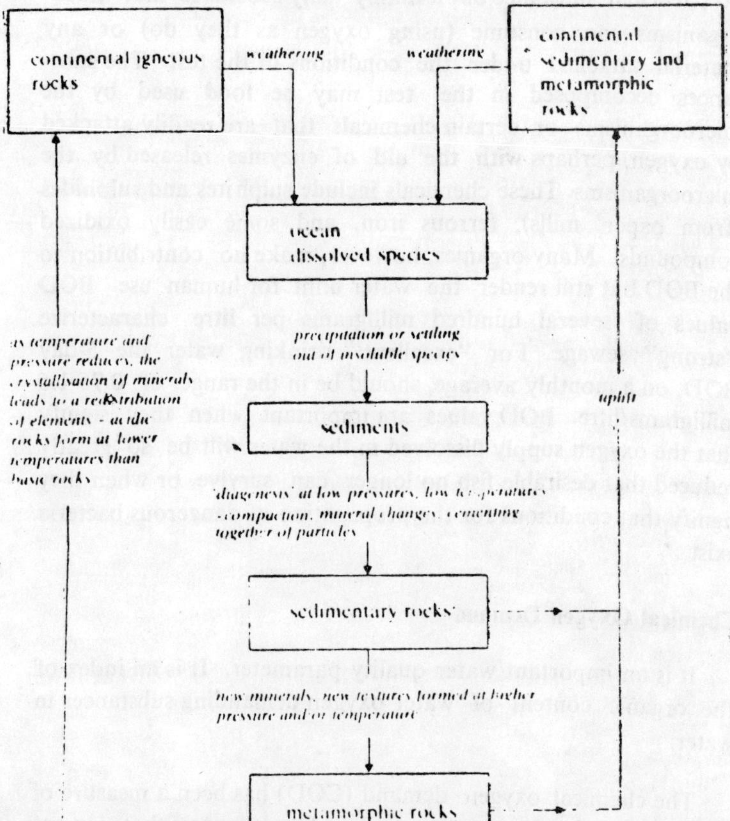

Fig. 1.6. Geological processes involved in geochemical cycles

no particular substance but a family—any substance that microorganisms can consume (using oxygen as they do) or any material attacked under the conditions of the test. The substances decomposed in the test may be food used by the microorganisms or certain chemicals that are readily attacked by oxygen, perhaps with the aid of enzymes released by the microorganisms. These chemicals include sulphites and sulphides (from paper mills), ferrous iron, and some easily oxidized compounds. Many organics, however, make no contribution to the BOD but still render the water unfit for human use. BOD values of several hundred milligrams per litre characterize "strong" sewage. For "excellent" drinking water the 5-day BOD, on a monthly average, should be in the range of 0.75-1.5 milligrams/litre. BOD values are important when they signify that the oxygen supply dissolved in the water will be so greatly reduced that desirable fish no longer can survive or when they signify that conditions for the propagation of dangerous bacteria exist.

Chemical Oxygen Demand

It is an important water quality parameter. It is an index of the organic content of water oxygen demanding substances in water.

The chemical oxygen demand (COD) has been a measure of the concentration in a water supply of substances that can get attacked by a strong chemical oxidizing agent in a standardized analysis. (Dichromate oxidation is commonly used). The results of the analysis are usually expressed in terms of the amount of oxygen that would be needed (in principle, because oxygen is not itself used) to oxidize the contaminants to the same final products obtained with the standardized analysis. COD values do not get necessarily correlated with BOD values. Textile wastes, paper mill wastes, and other wastes with high levels of cellulose have COD values considerably higher than their BOD values as cellulose is not readily attacked in the BOD test. Distillery and refinery wastes often have BODs higher than CODs unless the COD measurement is specially modified. In the nature of the two tests, the BOD of a given water supply is able to decrease faster than its COD.

Chemical oxygen demand (COD) has been found to be more scientific than the traditional empirical concept of Biological oxygen demand (BOD). The test is based on the chemical oxidation of material in water by $K_2Cr_2O_7$ in 50% H_2SO_4.

Pollutants

A pollutant may be defined as any thing, living or not living, or any physical agent (*e.g.*, heat, sound) that in its excess make any part of the environment undesirable; if water, undesirable; for drinking, recreation visual enjoyment, or as a habitat for the aquatic life normal to it; if air, undesirable for breathing, for the condition of buildings and monuments exposed to it, or for animal and plant life; if soil and land, undesirable for raising food and fiber, animals, or for recreation or aesthetic enjoyment. In common usage, "pollutant" is a term which is applied usually to non-living, man-made substances or other nuisances, and it refers to their being in excess in a particular location. Generally the same substances are produced by natural causes, and sometimes in far greater quantities. Oxides of sulphur and nitrogen, particulates and carbon monoxide, for example, all air pollutants, are all produced naturally. Generally, however, those made by nature get widely dispersed, are at low concentrations, and are not by themselves principal threats in congested urban areas. The excesses produced by human activities are the threats.

According to "The Indian Environment (Protection), Act 1986", a pollutant has been defined as any solid, liquid or gaseous substance present in such concentration as may be or tend to be injurious to environment.

Further, the unserviceable or residues of things which we manufacture, use and throw away are also regarded as pollutants.

Types of Pollutants

Certain common pollutants of well-developed and developing countries are as follows :

(i) Gaseous pollutants. Oxides of nitrogen (particularly, nitric oxide, No; nitrogen dioxide, NO_2) SO_2, H_2S, CO, halogens (chlorine, bromine, iodine), etc.

(ii) Fluoride compounds.

(iii) Metals. Mercury, lead, iron, zinc, nickel, tin, cadmium, etc.

(iv) Complex organic pollutants. Benzene, benzpyrene, acetic acid, ether, etc.

(v) Photochemical oxidants. Ozone, PAN, $PBzN_5$, NO_x, aldehyde, etylene etc.

(vi) Deposited matter. Soot, smoke tar, dust, grit.

(vii) Solid waste.

(viii) Economic poisons. Herbicides, fungicides, pesticides, nematocides, insecticides, rodenticides and other biocides.

(ix) Fertilisers.

(x) Radioactive waste.

(xi) Noise.

(xii) Heat.

However, from the ecosystem viewpoint, the pollutants can be classified into two basic types : nondegradable pollutants and biodegradable pollutants (Odum, 1971). The materials and poisons, like aluminium cans, mercurial salts, long-chain phenolic chemicals and DDT that either do not degrade or degrade only very slowly in the natural environment, are termed as nondegradable pollutants. Such nondegradable pollutants not only accumulate but are often "biologically magnified" as they move in biogeochemical cycles and along food chains. Also they frequently react with other compounds in the environment to produce additional toxins. The biodegradable pollutants include domestic sewage, heat, etc. The domestic sewage can get rapidly decomposed by natural processes or in engineered systems (like a municipal sewage treatment plant) that enhance nature's great capacity to decompose and recycle. Problems arise with the biodegradable pollutants when their input into the environment get exceeded the decomposition or dispersal capacity.

Natural and Man-Generated Pollution

Many pollutants that concern man occur in nature, although chlorinated hydrocarbons (such as DDT) and certain short-lived radioactive isotopes have been exceptions. In some cases, the environmental levels have been largely due to natural sources, while in others the levels have been largely produced by man's activities. Table 1.2 gives many examples. Even when natural sources have been more important on a global scale, man-generated pollutants may be more important in urban and industrial areas where the adverse effects of pollution are most severe. It thus becomes important to distinguish between large-scale production of pollutants and local production over a few tens or hundreds of square kilometers.

Table 1.2

Natural Versus Man-generated Pollution

Almost completely man-generated
Chlorinated hydrocarbons (DDT, etc.)
Lead aerosols
Substantially man-generated
Oil on the oceans
Phosphates in running waters
Substantial contributions from natural sources
Hydrocarbons in the atmosphere
Radiation
Sulfure oxides in the atmosphere

1.9 Environmental Segments

It is convenient to subdivide environmental chemistry into areas involving the chemistry of the atmosphere, hydrosphere, lithiosphere and biosphere. All matter, from minerals in the outer layers of the earth's crust to relatively stable ions in the upper reaches of the atmosphere may be classified in one of these categories.

(1) Atmosphere

The atmosphere refers to the protective blanket of gases which are surrounding the earth. It is able to sustain life on earth and saves it from the hostile environment of outer space. It is able to absorb most of the cosmic rays from outer space and a major portion of the electromagnetic radiation from the sun. It is able to transmit only near ultraviolet, visible, near infrared radiation (300-2500 nm) and radio waves (0.10-40μ) while filtering out tissue-damaging ultraviolet radiation below about 300 nm.

The atmosphere is subdivided into different regions of varying with altitudes. The most simple division is that of the lower atmosphere extending upto approximately so kilometres above the earth's surface and the upper atmosphere, extending out into space.

The atmosphere plays a vital role in maintaining the heat balance of the earth by absorbing infrared radiation emitted by the sun and re-emitted from the earth.

The major components of the atmosphere include nitrogen and oxygen, while the minor components include argon, carbon dioxide and some trace gases.

The atmosphere has been the source of oxygen (essential of life on earth) and carbon dioxide (essential for plant photosynthesis). It also supplies nitrogen which nitrogen-fixing bacteria and ammonia-manufacturing plants use to yield chemically bound nitrogen essential for life. Furthermore, it has been a vital carrier of water from oceans to land, as part of the hydrologic cycle.

Unfortunately, with progress in science and technology, man is dumping waste materials into the atmosphere, which pose a serious problem for survial of mankind itself on earth.

Atmospheric chemistry varies a good deal with altitude, exposure to solar radiation, pollution load and other factors.

(2) Hydrosphere

It refers to water in its various forms. It includes all types of water resources such as oceans, seas, rivers, lakes, streams, reservoirs, glaciers, polar ice caps and ground water (*i.e.*, water below the earth's surface). For the study of environmental chemistry, however, liquid water and the chemistry of the chemical entities therein is of predominant importance.

About 97% of the earth's water supply lies in the oceans, while the high salt content does not allow its use for human consumption. Nearly 2% of the water resource gets locked in the polar ice caps and glaciers, while only 1% is found as fresh water (surface water – rivers, lakes, streams, and ground water) for human consumption and other uses.

The history of ancient civilizations such as growth and decline has been closely linked with the quantum of water supply. The major uses of water include irrigation (30%) and thermal power plants (50%), while other uses include domestic (7%) and industrial consumption (~12%).

The contamination of surface water takes place by pesticides and fertilizers in agricultural run-off water, human and animal wastes in sewage and industrial wastes. Water-borne diseases occurring due to sewage alone have killed millions of people in many developing countries.

The basis of the aquatic environmental chemistry is a proper understanding of the sources, transport, characteristics and chemical species of water.

(3) Lithosphere

It includes the outer parts of the solid earth. In general, the term refers to minerals encarentered in the earth's crust and to the complex and variable mixture of minerals, organic matter, water and air making up soil. In so far as environmental chemistry is concerned, the soil is probably the most significant part of the lithosphere.

(4) Biosphere

It refers to the realm of living organisms and their interactions with the environment, *viz.*, atmosphere, hydrosphere and lithosphere. It includes living organisms and the surroundings in which they can exist.

The biosphere as well as environment are influenced considerably by each other. Thus, the oxygen and carbon dioxide levels of the atmosphere are based entirely on the plant kingdom. Because of the fact, green plants alone have been more or less reponsible for the accumulation of oxygen in the atmosphere through photosynthesis and decay, the original atmosphere having been devoid of oxygen.

The biological world, in general, has been intimately related to energy flows in the environment and water chemistry.

The biosphere is in fluenced tremendously by the chemistry of the environment and in turn exerts a powerful influence upon the chemistry of most environment, especially the lithosphere and hydrosphere (Fig. 1.7).

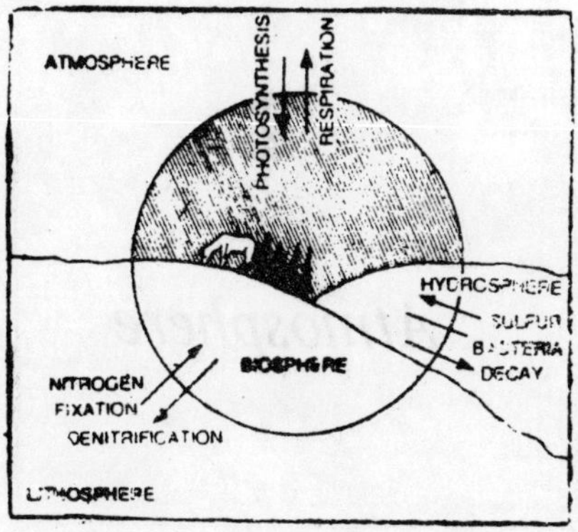

Fig. 1.7. Environmental Segments

2

Atmosphere

2.1 Introduction

We know that the trails of meteors as they enter the Earth's atmosphere have given us clues as to its composition. However since World War II, our knowledge of atmospheric chemistry, especially the upper atmosphere, has been enormously enlarged thanks to balloon, rocket, and instrument technology. In fact, it is probably not an exaggeration to say that our rocket and space programs have yielded just as much valuable information about the atmosphere of our own planet as about the Moon and other planets.

The atmosphere refers to a protective blanket which is able to nurture life on the earth and protects it from the hostile environment of outer space. It constitutes the source of carbon dioxide for plant photosynthesis and of oxygen for respiration. It provides the nitrogen which nitrogen-fixing bacteria and man's ammonia manufacturing plants employ to produce chemically bound nitrogen essential for life. As a basic component of the hydrologic cycle the atmosphere transports water from the oceans to land, thereby acting as the condenser in a vast solar-powered still. Unfortunately, the atmosphere also has been a dumping ground for many pollutant materials—ranging from sulfur dioxide to aerosol can Freon—a practice which causes damage to vegetation and materials, shortens human life, and possibly alters the characteristics of the atmosphere itself.

The atmosphere forms an insulating blanket around the earth. Without it the temperature at the equator would rise to 180° during the day and drop as low as −220°F at night. It burns up meteors that would bombard the surface of the earth from space. Without the atmosphere there would be no sound and no flight. There would be no conventional long-distance radio communication, for this is dependent on the electrons in the upper atmosphere. Without air there would be no lightning, no clouds, no wind, no rain, no snow, and no fire. The surface of the earth would be as bleak and sterile as the moon.

The atmosphere serves a vital protective function. It absorbs most of the cosmic rays from outer space and protects living things from their effects. It absorbs most of the electromagnetic radiation from the sun. Only radiation in the wavelength regions of 300 to 2500 nm and 0.01 to 40 m gets transmitted to any appreciable extent by the atmosphere. The first region consists of near-ultraviolet, visible, and near-infrared radiation; the second consists of radio waves. One segment is the optical window, consisting essentially of the visible spectrum of light, from near-ultraviolet to near-infrared. The other is the radio window, consisting of radio waves from about 1 centimetre to 40 metres in length. It is particularly fortunate for life on earth that the atmosphere filters cut tissue-damaging ultraviolet radiation below about 300 nm.

The atmosphere has been essential in maintaining the heat balance of the earth. The atmosphere absorbs infrared radiation emitted by the sun. It also absorbs energy re-emitted from the earth in the form of infrared radiation. Therefore it serves an important heat stabilizing function and prevents the tremendous temperature extremes which occur on planets and moons lacking substantial atmospheres.

The most familiar portion of the atmosphere of course, the lowest layer or troposphere, which extends 8 to 12 km up above the Earth's surface. Air temperature in the troposphere decreases with height at an average rate of about 0.5°C/km (Miyake, 1965). Convection mixes the troposphere vigorously so that its chemical composition is homogeneous with respect to major constituents. As we ascend, the strong winds cease abruptly and the tempera ture remains fairly constant at about −55°C. As every air traveler knows, there is little turbulence in the lower stratosphere; however, there can be a strong constant wind, the "jet stream." Between 35 and 50 km, there is a temperature inversion with a "warm" layer at about 0°C around 50 km called the stratopause. Another inversion begins above 80 km and the temperature beings to rise steadily until at 400 to 500 km the temperature may be as high as 2000 to 3000°K. The region between 80 and 400 to 500 km is generally known to be the thermosphere, the heterosphere, and the ionosphere. The warming of air near the Earth's surface is because of the absorption of solar energy by the more dense atmosphere and radioactive and conductive heating from the ground, that in turn is heated by the absorption of solar energy from without and by the heat from radioactive decay within. The maximum temperature in the stratosphere is due to the absorption of solar ultraviolet rays by ozone and molecular oxygen, while more serious chemical reactions produced by ionizing solar radiation are the reasons of the warming of the thermosphere.

It is impossible to define the limits of the atmosphere because the atmosphere becomes progressively tenuous with increasing distance from the earth. There is no boundary between the atmosphere and the void of outer space. However, 75 per cent of the earth's atmosphere lies within 10 miles of the surface and 99 per cent of the atmosphere lies below an. altitude of 30 kilometers (19 miles). The total mass has been estimated at 5,500 trillion tons.

2.2 Evolution of the Atmosphere

The atmosphere is the most changeable, and its changes are the most rapid, depending not only on terrestrial position and influences but upon the position of the Sun and upon the details of that star's activities. To deal with the complexity of the atmosphere and the rapid accummulation of data about it, a number of different systems of nomenclature have been proposed over the past several years.

It is now widely accepted that the earth's atmosphere originally was very different from its present state, and that the changes were brought about by biological activity.

Nearly 3.5 billion years ago when the first primitive life molecule got formed, the atmosphere was chemically reducing, having primarily methane, ammonia, water vapor, and hydrogen. The atmosphere was bombarded by intense, bond-breaking ultraviolet light. This light, along with lightning and radiation from radionuclides, provided the energy to bring about chemical reactions which caused the production of relatively complicated molecules, including even amino acids and sugars.

From the rich chemical mixture in the sea, life molecules got evolved. Initially these very primitive life forms derived their energy from fermentation of organic matter formed by chemical and photochemical processes, out eventually they gained the capability to produce organic matter, "CH_2O", by photosynthesis.

$$CO_2 + H_2O + h\nu \rightarrow CH_2O + O_2 \uparrow \quad (2.1)$$

and the stage was set for the massive biochemical transformation which caused the production of all the atmosphere's oxygen.

The life forms might have been blue-green algae whose limy deposits have been occurred in the oldest of Pre-Cambrian rocks. They were assumed to be first authentic members of the plant world (1400 million years ago). Probably, there was some oxygen which was essential to support the primitive life form. This presumably got formed in the upper atmosphere by the breakdown of water vapour by electrical discharge and solar radiation. The first plant and similar species might be the earth's first mass-producers of free O_2. When the supply of O_2 got increased more complex plants got evolved and accelerated the process

$$\text{Decaying Plants} \xrightarrow{CO_2} \text{sea} \xrightarrow{O_2} \text{Atmosphere}$$

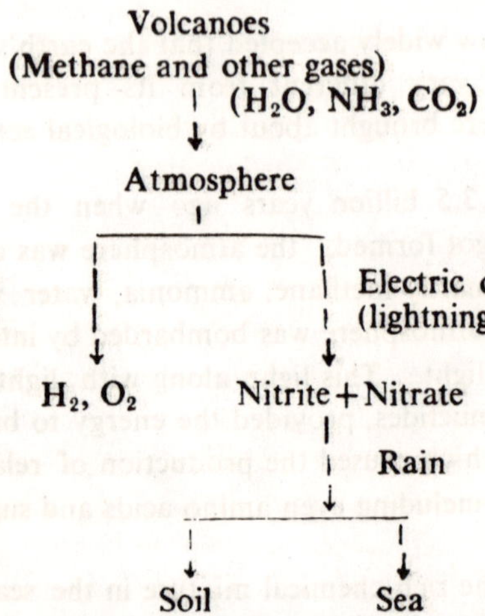

which got stepped up for millions of years, accompained by an enormous increase in O_2 – consuming animals to help maintain the O_2 - balance. The present composition of the atmosphere has been virtually the same as it was in the Cambrian age (500 million years ago). But it has been continually changing. The mobile gases of which it has been composed are always being absorbed by the soil, the rocks and living things or lost into outer space. The supply of atmospheric CO_2 is to be replenished every 4 to 8 years, O_2 every 3000 years and N_2, every 100 million years. The cycle of use and renewal of the atmospheric gases depicts an intriguing balance involving soil, air, animals and plants. It is to be noted that all living things have been mainly made of the elements of air; O_2, H_2O, C and N.

The oxygen initially produced by photosynthesis was probably quite toxic to primitive life forms. However, much of this oxygen got converted to iron oxides

$$4Fe^{2+} + O_2 + 4H_2O = 2Fe_2O_3 + 8H^+ \qquad .. (2.2)$$

by reaction with soluble iron (II). This caused the formation of enormous deposits of iron oxides, which provide major evidence for the liberation of free oxygen in the primitive earth atmosphere.

Eventually enzyme systems developed which enabled organisms to mediate the reaction of waste product oxygen with oxidizable organic matter in the sea. Later this made of waste product disposal was used by organisms for producing energy by respiration, which is now the primary mechanism by which most organisms obtain energy.

Eventually oxygen got accumulated in the atmosphere. This of course provided an abundant source of oxygen for respiration. It was having an additional benefit in that it enabled the formation of an ozone shield. This ozone shield absorbs bond-rupturing ultraviolet light. With the ozone shield protecting tissue from destruction by high energy ultraviolet radiation, the earth became a much more hospitable environment for life, and life forms were enabled to move from the sea to land.

2.3 The Earth's Heat Balance

The energy from the sun reaching the earth's upper atmosphere amounts to a very large quantity per unit time, a phenomenon which eventually may form the basis of a large solar energy industry. At the distance of the earth from the sun, a square metre of area perpendicular to the line of solar flux receives 19.2 kcal of energy per minute (Fig. 2.1). It has been

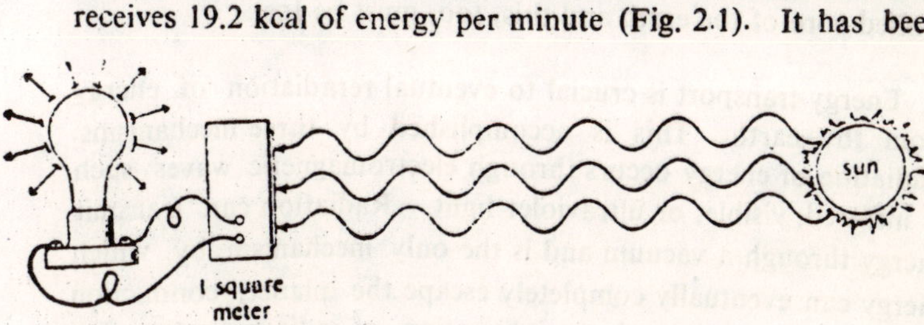

Fig. 2.1. The solar flux at the distance of the earth from the sun is 1.34×10^3 watts/m²

1.34×10^3 watts/m^2. The rate at which the sun's energy reaches the earth's atmosphere is termed as the solar constant.

If all of this energy reached the earth's surface and were retained, our planet would got vaporized long ago. As it is, the complex factors involved in maintaining the earth's heat balance within very narrow confines have been crucial to retaining conditions of climate which will support present levels of life on the earth. The great changes of climate which resulted in the ice ages were caused by variations of only a few degrees in average temperature. Marked climate changes within recorded history have been caused by average temperature changes of much less. The mechanisms by which the earth's average temperature has been retained within a narrow range are complex and not completely understood, but the main features will be explained here.

About 50% of the solar radiation incident to the earth reaches the earth's surface either directly or after scattering by clouds, atmospheric gases or particles. The remaining half of the incident radiation is either reflected directly from the atmosphere, or absorbed in the atmosphere and radiated back into space at a later time. Most of the solar energy reaching the earth's surface is absorbed and it must be returned to space to maintain the heat balance. In addition, a very small amount of energy (less than 1% of that received from the sun) reaches the earth's surface after arising from radioactive processes in the molted core of the earth and this, too, must be lost.

Energy transport is crucial to eventual reradiation of energy from the earth. This is accomplished by three mechanisms. Radiation of energy occurs through electromagnetic waves such as infrared, visible, or ultraviolet light. Radiation can transmit energy through a vacuum and is the only mechanism by which energy can eventually completely escape the planet, conduction of energy occurs through the interaction of adjacent atoms or molecules without the bulk movement of matter. Convection involves the movement of whole masses of air, which may be either relatively warm or cold. It is the phenomenon which can turn a balmy March morning into a frigid afternoon when a mass of cold arctic air moves into the vicinity. As well as carrying sensible heat due to the kinetic energy of molecules, convection carries latent heat, such as water vapor which releases heat as it condenses. An appreciable fraction of the earth's surface heat is transported to clouds in the atmosphere by conduction and convention before being lost ultimately by radiation.

The radiation which carries energy away from the earth is of a much longer wavelength than the sunlight which brings it to the earth. This is a crucial factor in maintaining the heat balance and one susceptible to upset by man's activities. The maximum intensity of incoming radiation occurs at 0.5 microns (500 nanometers) in the visible region with essentially none below 0.2 μ or above 3 μ. This encompasses the whole visible region and small parts of the ultraviolet and infrared adjacent to it. Outgoing radiation is in the infrared region with maximum intensity at about 10 μ and primarily between 2 and 40 μ. Thus the earth loses energy by electromagnetic radiation of much longer wavelength (lower energy) than the radiation by which it receives energy.

The average surface temperature of the earth is maintained at a relatively comfortable 15°C because water vapor, and to a lesser extent carbon dioxide, reabsorbs much of the outgoing radiation while retaining part of the energy as heat before eventual total loss. If this were not the case the earth's surface temperature would average around −40°C. Most of the absorption of infrared radiation is done by water molecules in the atmosphere. Absorption is weak in the regions 7 to 8.5 μ and 11 to 14 μ and nonexistent between 8.5 μ and 11 μ allowing a hole in the infrared absorption spectrum through which radiation may escape. Carbon dioxide, though present at a much lower concentration than water, absorbs strongly between 12 μ and 16.3 μ, and plays a key role in maintaining the heat balance. There is concern that an increase in the carbon dioxide level in the atmosphere could prevent sufficient energy loss to cause a perceptible and damaging increase in the earth's temperature.

This is the well-known, "greenhouse effect" which might result from elevated CO_2 levels coming from increased use of fossil fuels. The earth's radiation budget is illustrated.

2.4 Composition of the Atmosphere

The components of the atmosphere may be divided somewhat arbitrarily into major, minor and trace constituents. These components expressed for pollution-free dry air at ground level are given in Table 2.1.

Table 2.1

Components in Pollution-Free Dry Air at Ground Level Expressed as Per cent by Volume

Major components	*Volume per cent*
nitrogen	78.08
oxygen	20.95
Minor components	
argon	9.34×10^{-1}
carbon dioxide	3.14×10^{-2}
Trace components	
neon	1.818×10^{-3}
helium	5.24×10^{-4}
methane	2×10^{-4}
krypton	1.14×10^{-4}
nitrous oxide	2.5×10^{-5}
hydrogen	5×10^{-5}
xenon	$0-8.7 \times 10^{-6}$
sulfur dioxide	$0-1 \times 10^{-4}$
ozone	$0-2 \times 10^{-6}$
nitrogen dioxide	$0-2 \times 10^{-6}$
ammonia	0—trace
carbon monoxide	0—trace
iodine	0—trace

In addition to the components in Table 2.1, air may be having from 0.1 to 5 per cent water on a volume basis, with a normal range of 1 to 3 per cent. The density of the atmosphere decreases sharply with increasing altitude as a consequence of the gas laws and gravity. Over 99 per cent of the total mass of the atmosphere is found within approximately 30 km (1 km = 0.62 miles) of the earth's surface. The total mass of the atmosphere is nearly 5.5×10^{15} tons. Large as it is, this enormous mass has been only approximately one millionth of the earth's total mass.

The characteristics of the atmosphere have been found to vary greatly, particularly with altitude. Other factors introducing variability include season, latitude, time and even solar activity. Temperatures in the atmosphere may vary from as low as 138°C to over 1700°C. Atmospheric pressure drops from 1.00 atm at sea level to 3.0×10^{-7} atm at 100 km above sea level. Due to these variations, the chemistry of the atmosphere varies greatly with altitude. In addition to temperature differences, the mean free path of species in the atmosphere (mean distance travelled before collision with another particle) increases over many orders of magnitude with increasing altitude. A particle having a mean free path of approximately 1×10^{-6} cm at sea level is having a mean free path which is exceeding 2×10^{6} cm at an altitude of 500 km.

2.5 Oxygen in Atmosphere

Abundance by weight Earth, 28.5%; crust 46.6%; ocean, total 85.8%, dissolved O_2 6 ppm at 15°C; atmosphere, 23.2% ppm = mg kg^{-1}.

Oxygen has an distructively important place in the composition of both the animate and inanimate world. It is the only element which is present in high concentrations in the crust, atmosphere, hydrosphere and biosphere. Due to this reason oxygen deserves special consideration.

The majority of the oxygen in the Earth's crust is known to be chemically inert, and it remains bound to the same central atom in an oxyanion and experience the minimum of chemical change as it go through the geochemical cycle (Fig. 2.2).

The oxygen is chemically reactive in the atmosphere.

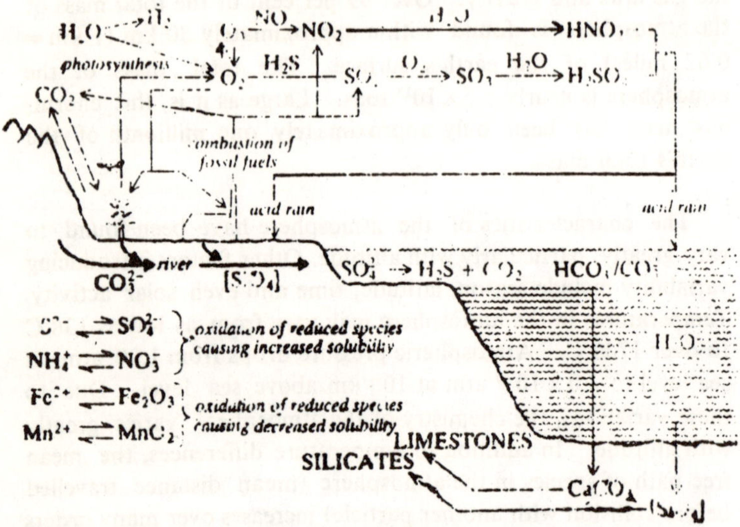

Fig. 2.2. Chemical species found in the oxygen cycle

2.6 Molecular Oxygen in the Atmosphere

Dioxygen. The existance of dioxygen in the atmosphere means that the reactions taking place on the Earth's surface are mainly carried out in oxidising conditions. One of the evidence which suggests that the early atmosphere did not contain dioxygen is the presence of pyrites, FeS_2, in sedimentary rocks formed by deposition in contact with the atmosphere. Presently oxidation reactions (Eqns. 2.3 and 2.4) tend to occur. These two equations can be combined into one (Eqn. 2.5) to give the overall reaction.

$$2FeS_2 + 7O_2 + 2H_2O \longrightarrow 2Fe^{2+} + 4SO_4^{2-} + 4H^+ \quad (2.3)$$

$$4Fe^{2+} + O_2 + 4H^+ \longrightarrow 4Fe^{3+} + 2H_2O \quad (2.4)$$

$$4FeS_2 + 15O_2 + 2H_2O \longrightarrow 4Fe^{3+} + 8SO_4^{2-} + 4H^+ \quad (2.5)$$

The oxygen is mainly present in the form of the dioxygen molecule, O_2. The reactivity of dioxygen is large enough to have a controlling influence on the geochemical cycles of many other elements, like carbon, hydrogen, nitrogen, sulphur and iron. As it has already been mentioned that the majority of the dioxygen in the atmosphere is being produced by photosynthesis. In addition, a small amount is produced by the action of ultraviolet (UV) light on water molecules in the upper regions of the atmosphere. This reaction (Eqn. 2.6) is said to be photodissociation, and the hydrogen produced escapes into space.

$$2H_2O \xrightarrow{\text{UV light}} 2H_2+O_2 \qquad (2.6)$$

Ultraviolet radiation is also involved in the conversion of dioxygen into the triatomic molecule ozone, O_3. This reaction (Eqn. 2.7) is called photolysis and is of special importance because the ozone has the ability to absorb ultraviolet radiation.

$$O_2 \xrightarrow{\text{UV light}} O+O \text{ (atomic oxygen)} \qquad (2.7)$$

$$O+O_2 \longrightarrow O_3 \qquad (2.8)$$

Respiration (Eqn. 2.9) is used mostly by all the organisms as a means of producing energy; this reaction combined with the oxidation of dead organic matter (a chemically similar react'on) reverses the photosynthetic process.

$$\underset{\text{Carbohydrate}}{(CH_2O)n}+\underset{\text{dioxygen}}{nO_2} \longrightarrow \underset{\text{Carbon dioxide}}{nCO_2}+\underset{\text{water}}{nH_2O} \qquad (2.9)$$

The burning of fossil fuels also produces carbon dioxide and water at the cost of dioxygen, but this is just a delayed oxidation of dead organic matter. Hydrogen sulphide, H_2S, from volcanoes and organic decay, is converted to sulphur dioxide, SO_2, in the atmosphere. This sulphur dioxide, plus that produced by the combustion of fossil fuels and the extraction of metals from sulphide, ores, is eventually converted to sulphate, SO_4^{2-} and comes back to the Earth's surface, often as acid rain. Like wise the various oxides of nitrogen, either produced by micro-organisms or by human activities, are eventually converted to to nitrate, NO_3^-, and can also produce acid rain. The phrase 'anthropogenic sources' is often used to show that something is being produced by human activities. On land, and to a smaller extent in the oceans, many metals are converted to insoluble oxides (Eqn. 2.10) by atmospheric dioxygen, but some other reduced species generally compounds of non-metals) are oxidised to more soluble forms (Eqn. 2.11).

$$4\,Fe^{-2} + 3O_2 \longrightarrow 2Fe_2O_3 \qquad (2.10)$$

reduced forms	iron (II) (soluble)	iron (III) oxide (insoluble)	oxidised forms

$$S^{2-} + 2O_2 \longrightarrow SO_4^{2-} \qquad (2.11)$$

sulphide (insoluble)	sulphate (soluble)

At present there seems to be a state of equilibrium between the rate of utilisation of dioxygen in the atmosphere the rate of its formation. This indicates that there are very rapid feedback mechanisms in the system that counterbalance any changes in rates of formation or removal. The feedback mechanism is probably linked to the carbon cycle and the amount of organic matter included the ocean sediments. If the concentration of dioxygen is lowered more carbon is incorporated in the sediments, *i.e.*, photosynthesis is increased compared to removal processes; if the concentration of dioxygen rises, less carbon is incorporated in the sediments, *i.e.*, removal processes are increased compared to photosynthesis.

2.7 Photosynthesis

Photosynthesis is one of the most important step in the oxygen cycle. Not only is dioxygen produced—dioxygen which is consumed by humans and other animals to liberate the energy necessary for life by oxidising organic chemicals – but the organic chemicals themselves are derived from the carbon used in the photosynthesis reaction (Eqn. 2.12)

$$nCO_2 + nH_2O \xrightarrow{\text{light}} (CH_2O)n + nO_2 \qquad (2.12)$$

carbon dioxide — water — carbo-hydrate — dioxygen

Water which is the most common hydrogen donor, with the hydrogen which is transferred to the carbon atoms obtained from the carbon dioxide, and the oxygen from the water being liberated as dioxygen. The photosynthetic reaction occurs only in the presence of light. The light energy which is absorbed by green plants and get converted into chemical energy is stored in the bonds of the organic chemicals formed. For example the production of 180g of glucose (1 mole of glucose) requires an energy input of 2880 kJ at 25°C and 1 atmosphere pressure. This energy can be released by breaking down the glucose molecule by reaction with dioxygen (Eqn. 2.13). The process is said to be aerobic respiration.

$$C_6H_{12}O_6 + 6O_2 \longrightarrow 6CO_2 + 6H_2O + \text{energy} \qquad (2.13)$$

glucose

Green plants contain chlorophyll molecules that are capable of absorbing some of the visible part of the electromagnetic radiation emitted by the sun. The energy in this absorbed radiation raises. The energy of some electrons in the chlorophyll molecules is raised because of the energy of the absorbed radiation. These excited electrons are then donated to an electron acceptor which initiates a series of electron-transfer reactions which ultimately leads to the formation of carbohydrates, like glucose. The light energy is being absorbed at two stages in the photosynthesis process and raises the energy of electrons. The electrons cannot be continuously removed from the chlorophyll molecules without being replaced. In plants and blue-green algae, water is responsible for the replacement electrons (Eqn. 2.14), dioxygen is evolved and the protons eventually combine with carbon.

$$2H_2O \rightleftharpoons 2H^+ + 2OH^- \longrightarrow 4H^+ + O_2 + 4e^- \qquad (2.14)$$

Chlorophyll mainly absorbs red and blue light, so the light reflected contains mainly the unabsorbed green light. Due to this reason only the leaves containing chlorophyll appear green.

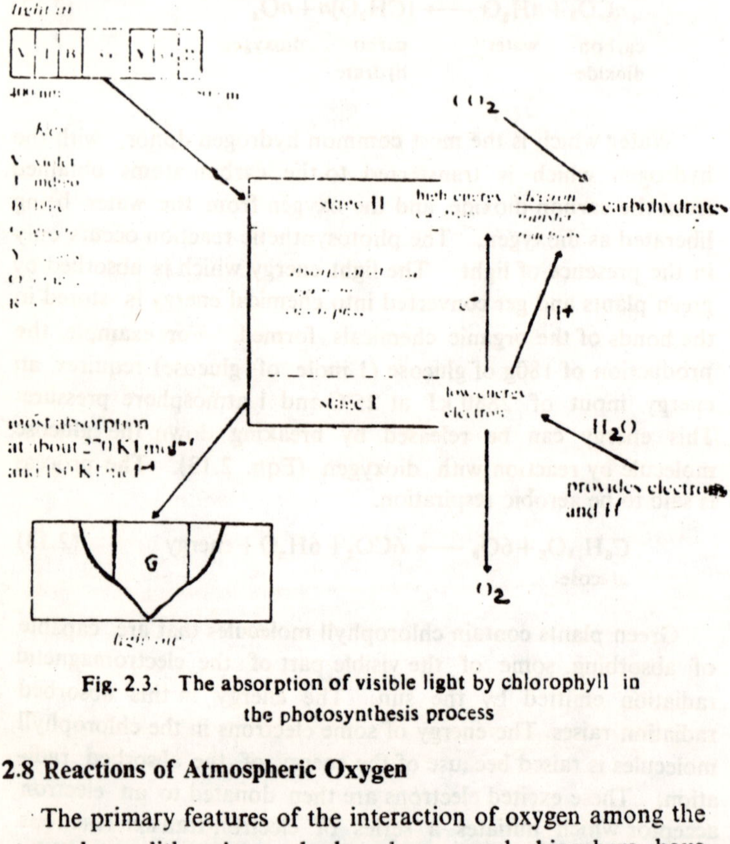

Fig. 2.3. The absorption of visible light by chlorophyll in the photosynthesis process

2.8 Reactions of Atmospheric Oxygen

The primary features of the interaction of oxygen among the atmosphere, lithosphere, hydrosphere, and biosphere have already been given. The oxygen cycle is critically important in atmospheric chemistry, geochemical transformations, and life processes.

Oxygen in the troposphere plays a vital role in processes on the earth's surface. Atmospheric oxygen takes part in energy-producing reactions, like the burning of fossil fuels

$$CH_4\text{(in natural gas)} + 2O_2 = CO_2 + 2H_2O$$

Atmospheric oxygen is used by aerobic organisms in the degradation of organic material :

$$CH_2O+O_2 \xrightarrow{\text{organisms}} CO_2+H_2O$$

Some oxidative weathering processes, like consume oxygen.

$$4FeO+O_2 \longrightarrow 2Fe_2O_3$$

Oxygen gets returned to the atmosphere through the photosynthetic reactions of plants :

$$CO_2+H_2O \xrightarrow{\text{plants}} CH_2O+O_2$$

Due to the extremely rarefied atmosphere and the effects of ionizing radiation, oxygen in the upper atmosphere exists in some forms which are quite different from those stable at lower levels. In addition to molecular oxygen, O_2, the upper atmosphere is having oxygen atoms, O; excited oxygen molecules, O_2^*; and ozone, O_3.

Atomic oxygen, O, is stable primarily in the thermosphere where the atmosphere has been so rarefied that the three-body collisions necessary for the chemical reaction of atomic oxygen seldom take place. Atomic oxygen is produced by a photochemical reaction :

$$O_2+h\nu \rightarrow O+O$$

Ultraviolet radiation in the wavelength regions 135 nm to 176 nm, and 240 nm to 260 nm has been most effective in causing the above Reaction to occur. Due to photochemical dissociation, molecular oxygen, O_2, is virtually nonexistent at very high altitudes. At altitudes exceeding about 80 km the average molecular weight of air is lower than the 28.97 g/mole observed at sea level due to the high concentration of atomic oxygen resulting from photochemical dissociation of O_2. The resulting division of the atmosphere between a lower section with a uniform molecular weight and a higher region with a nonuniform molecular weight forms the basis for classifying two atmospheric regions as the homosphere and heterosphere, respectively. Less than 10% of the oxygen in the atmosphere at altitudes exceeding approximately 400 km is present as O_2.

Atomic oxygen is partially responsible for the phenomenon : known as airglow. Excited atomic oxygen, O*, gives out visible light at wavelengths of 636 nm, 630 nm, and 558 nm. This species is formed by reactions such as the following :

$$O+O+O \rightarrow O_2, O^*$$

Airglow is a very faint electromagnetic radiation which is continuously emitted by the earth's atmosphere. Although the visible component of airglow is extremely weak, the phenomenon is quite intense in the infrared region of the spectrum.

Oxygen ions, O^+, may be formed by ultraviolet radiation acting upon oxygen atoms :

$$O + h\nu \rightarrow O^+ + e$$

O^+ is the predominant positive ion in some regions of the ionosphere. It may undergo the following reactions to form other important positive ions :

$$O^+ + O_2 \rightarrow O_2^+ + O$$
$$O^+ + N_2 \rightarrow NO^+ + N$$

In intermediate regions of the ionosphere, the species O_2^+ is formed by absorption of ultraviolet radiation at wavelengths of 17 nm to 103 nm. The reaction

$$O_2 + h\nu = O_2^+ + e$$

may also be energized by soft X-rays. The reaction

$$N_2^+ + O_2 = N_2 + O_2^+$$

also give rise to O_2^+ in this region.

Ozone, O_3, is an extremely significant oxygen-containing species occurring in the stratosphere. Ozone absorbs harmful ultraviolet radiation and serves as a radiation shield protecting living beings on the earth from the effects of excessive amounts

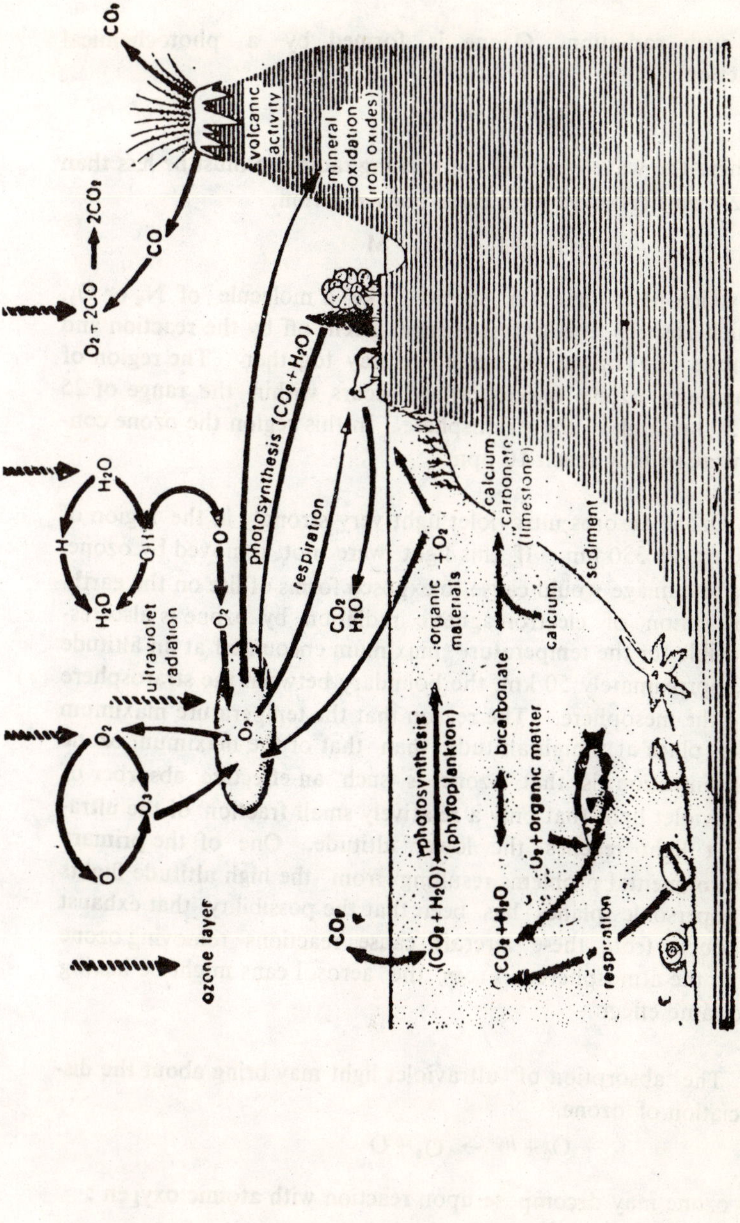

Fig. 2.4. Oxygen cycle (after Herreid II, 1977)

of such radiation. Ozone is formed by a photochemical reaction

$$O_2 + h\nu \rightarrow O + O$$

(where the wavelength of the exciting radiation must be less than 242.4 nm) followed by a three-body reaction,

$$O + O_2 + M \rightarrow O_3 + M$$

in which M is another species, like a molecule of N_2 or O_2, which absorbs the excess energy given off by the reaction and enables the ozone molecule to stay together. The region of maximum ozone concentration occurs within the range of 25 to 30 km high in the stratosphere. In this region the ozone concentration may reach 10 ppm.

Ozone absorbs ultraviolet light very strongly in the region of 220 nm to 330 nm. If this light were not removed by ozone, severe damage would cause to exposed forms of life on the earth. Absorption of electromagnetic radiation by ozone is also responsible for the temperature maximum encounted at an altitude of approximately 50 km, the boundary between the stratosphere and the mesophere. The reason that the temperature maximum takes place at a high altitude than that of the maximum ozone concentration is that ozone is such an effective absorber of ultraviolet light that only a relatively small fraction of the ultraviolet light reaches the lower altitude. One of the primary environmental problems resulting from the high altitude flights of supersonic planes has been that the possibility that exhaust products from these aircraft cause reactions removing ozone from the atmosphere. From the aerosol cans might be having the same effect.

The absorption of ultraviolet light may bring about the dissociation of ozone.

$$O_3 + h\nu \rightarrow O_2 + O$$

or ozone may decompose upon reaction with atomic oxygen :

$$O_3 + O \rightarrow O_2 + O_2$$

Atomic oxygen may also be eliminated by the following reaction :

$$O + O + M \rightarrow O_2 + M$$

2.9 Ozone

The electromagnetic radiation from the sun which falls on the upper layers of the atmosphere has much more ultraviolet light (*i.e.*, higher-energy radiation) compared to the radiation reaching to the land and water surface of the Earth (Fig. 2.5). The ultraviolet light contain enough energy to bring about a number of photochemical reactions (reactions induced by light) involving various forms of oxygen like ozone, O_3, and atomic oxygen, O. These reactions occur continuously. The equilibrium concentration of ozone and atomic oxygen is increased. As the concentration of dioxygen in the Earth's atmosphere is increased with the development of photosynthetic organisms. The increased levels of ultraviolet-absorbing species reduces the quantity of ultraviolet radiation reaching to the lower atmosphere. Low levels of ultraviolet radiation can cause skin cancer in humans and high levels are dangerous to most organisms. The continued absorption of the ultraviolet light by the species in the ozone layer 20—50 km above the Earth's surface is necessary for the survival of present life-forms.

The absorption of ultraviolet light in the 2000- to 32000-Å range by ozone is so large that the atmospheric ozone layer effectively prevents this radiation from reaching to the Earth's surface. While solar ultraviolet radiation may have played a role in prebiological chemical synthesis on this planet, it is highly lethal to complexly organized biomolecules. Thus ancient life forms could not leave the protective seas until photosynthesis had produced the oxygen from which in turn the ozone shield was formed.

The ozone concentration also depends on location. The concentration of ozone in the lower atmosphere is very low, very variable, and because of the presence of oxidizeable aerosols very transitory.

In larger, concentrations, ozone has an offensive, astringent, and unmistakable odor and is sometimes noticeable around electrical discharge machinery. Ozone can be a pollutant, and it can be produced in the troposphere by photochemical reactions of smog.

The level of ozone in the stratosphere is even less than ten parts per million (10 ppm) where the rate of formation is being balanced by the rate of removal, though daily there are variations of a few per cent about the mean values. As explained (Fig. 2.5), there are three important ozone-removal mechanisms in addition to the ultraviolet-initiated photochemical decomposition. The levels of nitrogen oxides could be raised by the increased use of nitrogen fertilisers and the combustion of fossil fuels at high temperatures. The introduction of supersonic aircraft which actually enter the stratosphere was viewed with special concern because they would directly inject nitrogen oxides into the ozone layer. Normally there is only slow transfer of material from the lower atmosphere (the troposphere) to the stratosphere. Direct injection into the stratosphere would bypass removal mechanisms operating in the troposphere. Luckily the number of supersonic aircraft are less than forecast and the effects have been minimised. Another danger to the ozone layer has been the use of chlorofluorocarbons (CCl_3F and CCl_2F_2) in aerosol-spray cans and as refrigerants, solvents, and foaming agents. These compounds are inert in the troposphere, but in the stratosphere they undergo photochemical decomposition giving rise to chlorins atoms which catalyse the decomposition of ozone (Equ. 2.15).

$$\underset{\text{dichlorodifluoromethane}}{CCl_2F_2} \xrightarrow{\text{UV light}} \underset{\text{activated chlorine atom}}{Cl} \xrightarrow{O_3} O_2 + \underset{\text{chlorine oxide}}{ClO} \xrightarrow{O} O_2 + \underset{\text{can react again}}{Cl} \quad (2.15)$$

There is a large amount of uncertainty about the actual effects of these human additions to natural processes, mainly because of the difficulties of making measurements and recognising whether variations in ozone levels are natural or not. Another problem is that the chlorofluorocarbons and nitrogen oxides from fertilisers are only slowly transferred to the

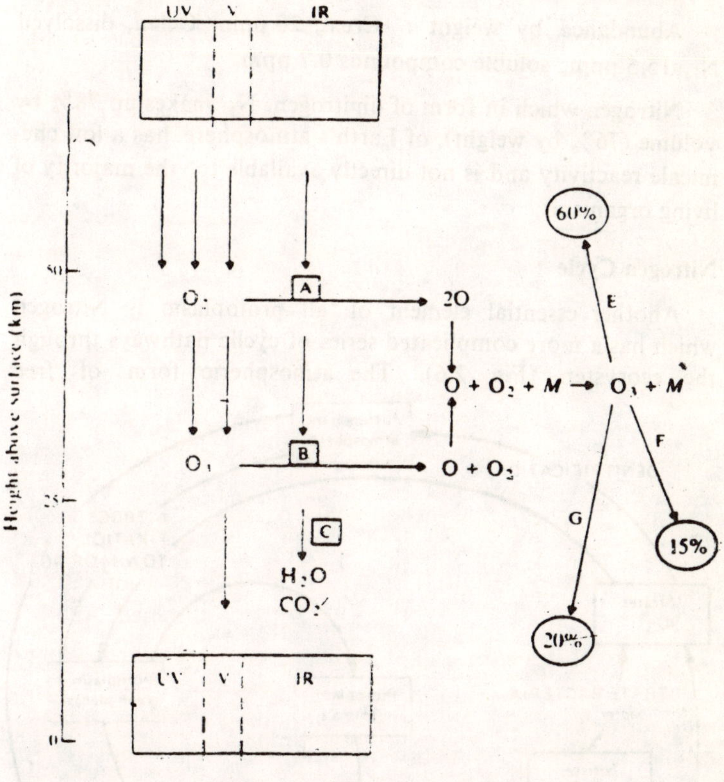

Key

A ultraviolet absorbed, < 242 nm

B ultraviolet absorbed, 200–300 nm

C infra-red absorbed

E (i) $NO + O_3 \rightarrow NO_2 + O_2$
(ii) $NO_2 + O \rightarrow NO + O_2$

F (i) $HO + O_3 \rightarrow HO_2 + O_2$
(ii) $HO_2 + O \rightarrow OH + O_2$

G $O + O_3 \rightarrow 2O_2$

n% percentage of natural removal rate

M a metallic species

Fig. 2.5. Natural ozone-removal mechanisms and the absorption of ultraviolet radiation by ozone in the Earth's atmosphere.

stratosphere, but the levels in the troposphere are high enough to cause possible ozone depletion for another 50 years !

2.10 Nitrogen in Atmosphere

Abundance by weight : Crust, 20 ppm; Oclan, dissolved N_2, 15.5 ppm; soluble compounds 0.7 ppm.

Nitrogen which in form of dinitrogen, N_2. makes up 78% by volume (76% by weight), of Earth's atmosphere has a low chemicale reactivity and is not directly available to the majority of living organisms.

Nitrogen Cycle

Another essential element of all protoplasm is Nitrogen which has a more complicated series of cyclic pathways through the ecosystem (Fig. 2.6). The atmospheric form of free

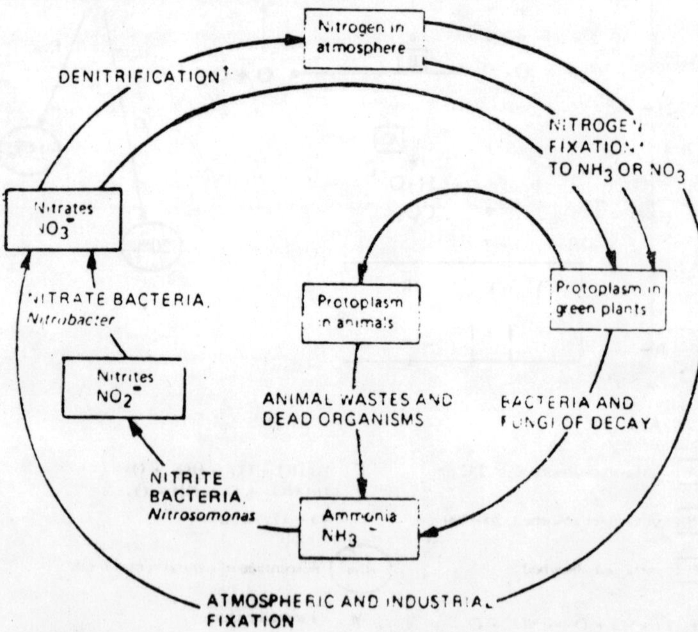

† *Denitrifying bacteria*
Pseudomonas
Thiobacillus
Micrococcus denitrificans

Nitrogen fixing bacteria and Algae
Free-living Azotobacter, Clostridium
Leguminous Rhizobium
Blue-green Nostoc, Anabaena

Fig. 2.6. Nitrogen Cycle

nitrogen must be "fixed"—incorporated into chemical compounds that can be used by plants, for example ammonia (NH_3). Nitrogen fixation is (performed successfully) by bac.erial action of both free-living soil bacteria like Azotobacter and Clostridium, and symbiotic bacteria such as Rhizobium, which live in root nodules of leguminous plants. Number of other bacteria can perform nitrogen fixation, and some blue-green algae like Anabaena and Nostoc can also accomplish this reaction. Nitrogen fixation can be achieved as a physical process in the atmosphere by the ionizing effect of lightning and cosmic radiation, or industrially through the Habar and Bosch method. The largest single source of fixed nitrogen, however, is probably terrestrial bacteria.

From the different forms of ammonia and soluble nitrates, plants incorporate fixed nitrogen into protoplasm by amino acid and protein synthesis. Then the organic nitrogen compounds can follow any one of three processes :

1. They may be stored or modified as proteins or nucleic acids within the plant;
2. They may be incorporated into animal protein through consumption and assimilation by animals; or
3. They may be decomposed to NH_3 through death and bacterial action. In animals, these compounds may also be metabolically decomposed into urea and other excretory products.

In the decomposition cycle through death and decay, ammonia (NH_3) is produced from amino acids by the action of ammonifying bacteria like Pseudomonas, Proteus, and so on. Under normal circumstances it is readily converted into nitrite form (NO_2) by nitrite bacteria like Nitrosomonas, and into nitrate from (NO_3) by nitrate bacteria such as Nitrobacter. Nitrates are then absorbed directly by plants as primary nutrients and incorporated once again into amino acids and proteins by organic synthesis within the plant.

The presence of ammonia nitrogen in ecosystems is a good measure of the balance between bacterial action, protein decomposition and plant production. High levels of ammonia nitrogen in water are usually indicative of enrichment from fertilizer, animal wastes, or domestic sewage. Thereby, field measurements of ammonia nitrogen above the levels of 1 ppm. usually show some major source of decomposition within the system, in excess of that being used by bacterial action and plant growth. Field measurements of nitrites and nitrates are also good indicators to the nutrient condition of lakes streams, and estuaries. As we will see lakes that the some if true for dissolved phosphates.

Nitrogen can come back to its atmospheric form by the action of denitrifying bacteria such as Pseudomonas, Thiobacillus, and Micrococcus denitrificans. It is obvious that the cyclic flow of nitrogen throughout the ecosystem requires balances of bacterial action involving many species, so that appropriate levels of plant nutrients are maintained without excessive accumulation of decomposition products like ammonia. A 1969 report on environmental problems by a committee of the American Chemical Society pointed out that all life could be extinguished on earth by the extinction of perhaps just a dozen species of bacteria involved in the nitrogen cycle.

2.11 Reactions of Atmospheric Nitrogen

The atmosphere contains 78% nitrogen by volume and constitutes an inexhustible reservoir of that essential element.

Unlike oxygen, which is almost completely dissociated to the monatomic form in higher regions of the thermosphere, molecular nitrogen is not readily dissociated by ultraviolet radiation. However, at altitudes exceeding approximately 100 km, atomic nitrogen is produced by photochemical reactions :

$$N_2 + h\nu \rightarrow N + N \qquad (2.1)$$

Other reactions which may produce monatomic nitrogen have been the following :

$$N_2^+ + O \rightarrow NO^+ + N \quad (2.2)$$

$$NO^+ + e \rightarrow N + O \quad (2.3)$$

$$O^+ + N_2 \rightarrow NO^+ + N \quad (2.4)$$

In one region of the ionosphere, the so-called E region, NO^+ has been one of the predominant ions. A plausible sequence of reactions by which NO^+ is formed is the following :

$$N_2 + h\nu = N_2^+ + e \quad (2.5)$$

$$N_2^+ + O = NO^+ + N \quad (2.6)$$

In the lowest region of the ionosphere, the D region which extends from approximately 50 km in altitude to approximately 85 km, NO^+ is formed directly by ionizing radiation :

$$NO + h\nu = NO^+ + e \quad (2.7)$$

In the lower part of the D region the ionic species N_2^+ is formed through the action of galactic cosmic rays :

$$N_2 + h\nu = N_2^+ + e \quad (2.8)$$

Pollutant oxides of nitrogen, particularly NO_2, are key species involved in air pollution and the formation of photochemical smog. For example, NO_2 is readily dissociated photochemically to NO and reactive atomic oxygen :

$$NO_2 + h\nu = NO + O \quad (2.9)$$

This reaction is the most important primary photochemical precen involved in smog formation.

2.12 Carbon Cycle

Carbon which is key element in all living organisms, cycles relatively simple among plants, animals, and the inorganic world. Fig. 2.7 depicts the common pathways of carbon in an ecosystem. This diagram is over-amplified because there are actually separate carbon cycles on land and in water, but they are almost similar and are dynamically corelated at the air-water interface.

Carbon is present in the atmosphere primarily as carbon dioxide, in which form it is incorporated directly into plant protoplasm in the phenomenon of photosynthesis. For instance a tropical rain forest may incorporate between one and two kilograms of carbon per square meter per annum into organic compounds. From plants, organic carbon can go into animals, where it goes through various stages of digestion and assimilation, and from either plants or animals it reenter in the atmosphere as CO_2 by respiration. If it remains is plants and animals, it at lost passes into dead organic material from which it can return to atmospheric CO_2 by oxidation or decomposition. In some animals, carbon can become tied up in hard parts such as shells, and thereby remain in the form

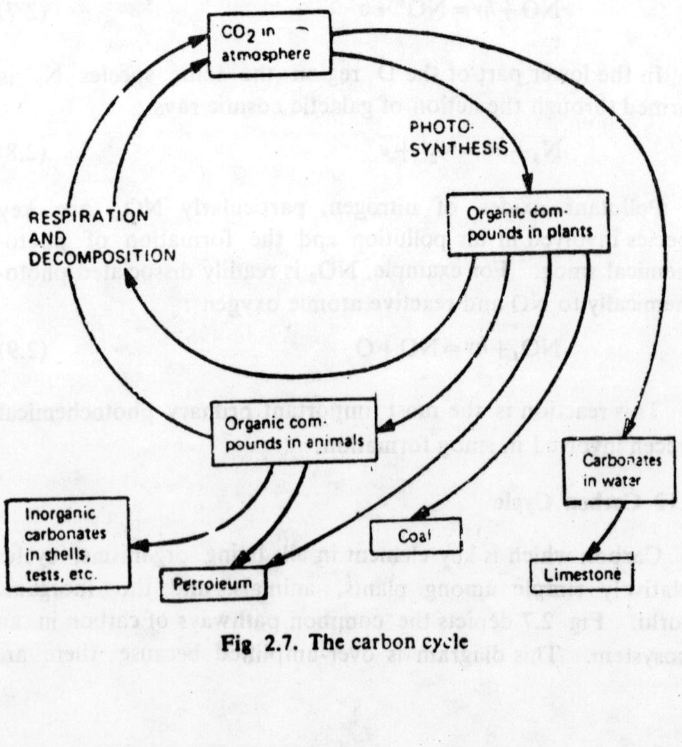

Fig 2.7. The carbon cycle

of inorganic carbonates for a long period time. Limestone may result from marine deposits of animal carbonates as well as from inorganic precipitation of carbonates in water. These carbonates in limestone may then return to the living carbon cycle only very slowly by the process of erosion and dissolution. Dissolved carbonates in water can be absorbed by plants—few aquatic plants, for example Eurasian milfoil may use the carbon in dissolved carbonates as a direct carbon source in photosynthesis. Most aquatic plants efficient enough in using free CO_2 in water as a carbon source.

Carbon can also become "locked" in organic deposits of petroleum and coal, which remains in this form for millions of years unless it released in combustion. A detailed discussion of the carbon cycle has been presented in an issue of Scientific American devoted to the ecology of the biosphere. Some highlights of carbon cycles are shown below.

2.13 Atmospheric Carbon Dioxide

Carbon dioxide is composing only 0.0314 per cent by volume of the atmosphere. It is the nonpollutant species of most concern in the atmosphere. Carbon dioxide, along with water vapor, is mainly responsible for the absorption of infrared energy from the sun, and reradiation of this energy back to the earth's surface. There are some scientists which fear that changes in the atmospheric carbon dioxide level will bring about marked changes in the earth's climate through the greenhouse effect discussed in a separate chapter.

In terms of strictly chemical reactions in the atmosphere, carbon dioxide is a relatively insignificant species. It is present in relatively low concentrations and is not thought to participate significantly in photochemical reactions. The infrared radiation which it absorbs is not sufficiently energetic to cause chemical reactions.

2.14 The Formation of Carbon Compounds and Photosynthesis

Photosynthesis in a source of dioxygen and a means of storing solar energy as chemical energy.

The light is absorbed by a number of pigment molecules, the most abundant of which are chlorophyll *a* and *b*. In the plants which are higher, the pigments are concentrated in the green-tissue cells. There are two pigment systems in the green cells and each is responsible for absorbing particular region of the light spectrum.

System containing chlorophyll a absorbs red light ($\lambda \simeq 650$ nm) to give rise excited molecules containing electrons in higher energy states. These electrons are transferred to compounds like ATP or NADPH. The ATP transfers a phosphate group, to one of the organic reactants (Eqn. 2.16), that is then react in the desired manner (Eqn. 2.17). The addition of phosphate is said to be phosphorylation reaction.

$$\underset{\text{organic molecule}}{ROH} + ATP \longrightarrow \underset{\text{phosphorylated intermediate}}{ROPO_3} + \underset{\text{adenosine-5'-diphosphate}}{ADP} \qquad (2.16)$$

$$ROPO_3 \xrightarrow[\text{reaction}]{\text{further}} \underset{\text{organic phosphate product}}{ROX} + PO_4^{3/4} \qquad (2.17)$$

ATP behaves as an efficient energy-transfer agent. The energy can come directly from photosynthesis or from the chemical energy in compounds such as fats and carbohydrates which are broken down as required to regenerate ATP.

Nicotinamide adenine dinucleotide phosphate (NADPH) is reduced and acts as a carries of protons and electrons (Eqn. 218).

$$NADPH + \underset{\text{compound}}{\text{oxidised}} \longrightarrow NADP^+ + \underset{\text{products}}{\text{reduced}} \qquad (2.18)$$

The $NADP^+$ can generate the NADPH, nicotinamide adenine dinucleotide phosphate (Eqn 2.19)

$$NADP^+ + H^+ + 2e^- \longrightarrow NADPH \qquad (2.19)$$

During photosynthesis the electrons are protons are given by water with the release of dioxygen (Eqn. 2.20).

$$2H_2O \dashrightarrow O_2 + 4H^+ + 4e^- \quad (2.20)$$

The incorporation and reduction of carbon dioxide to form the various organic products of photosynthesis involves a complex series of cyclic reactions (fig. 2.8.) One molecule of carbon dioxide is added to an activated organic molecule. The product is then progressively reduced by NADPH, and rearranged, under the influence of enzymes, unless the final compound, whether a lipid or Carbohydrate protein is produced.

The consequences of photosynthesis are that the photo-autotrophs are net absorbers of carbon dioxide, water and sunlight, and net producers of organic molecules and dioxygen.

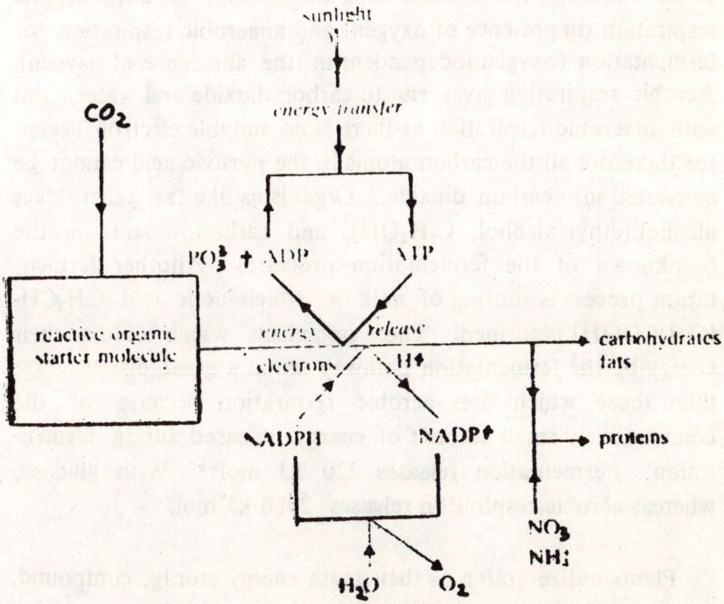

Fig. 2.8. The use of NADPH and ATP in a photosynthetic reaction sequence. (A diagrammatic representation)

2.15 Lipids and Carbohydrates

The two important groups of energy-storing chemicals produced in photosynthesis process are lipids and carbohydrates. One major source of biologically available energy is provided by the breakdown of monosaccharides like glucose. Whe dioxygen is present, the complete decomposition of the glucose to carbon dioxide and water can be achieved with the release of large amount of energy (2900 kJ/mole) accumulated during photosynthesis. The large portion of this energy is transferred inside the organism by the 38 molecules of ATP which are synthesised during this aerobic respiration. The first steps in the oxidation of glucose lead to the formation of pyruvic acid ($CH_3COCOOH$) and refflcient energy to generate two ATP molecules. The presence of dioxygen is not required up to this stage and the reaction steps are common to both aerobic respiration (in presence of oxygen) and anaerobic respiration or fermentation (oxygen-independent in the abrecence of oxygen). Aerobic respiration gives rise to carbon dioxide and water, but with anaerobic respiration as there is no suitable electron acceptor therefore all the carbon atoms in the pyruvic acid cannot be converted into carbon dioxide. Organisms like as yeast gives alcohol (ethyl alcohol, C_2H_5OH), and carbon dioxide in the best known of the fermentation processes. Another fermentation process is souring of milk in which lactic acid ($CH_3CH(OH)COOH$) is formed. Those organisms which obtain their energy by the fermentation pathway are at a great disadvantage than those which uses aerobic respiration because of the comparatively small amount of energy released during fermentation. Fermentation releases 220 kJ mol^{-1}. With glucose, whereas aerobic respiration releases 2900 kJ/mol.

Plants utilize starch as their main energy storage compound, but animals use fats. Fats, are more concentrated energy-storage compounds than carbohydrates.

2.16 Geochemical Accumulation of Solar Energy

In the process of photosynthesis plants and ultimately animals are provided with energy by converting solar energy into chemical energy. Any organic remains of dead plants and animals which have been buried in sediments can be considered as containing trapped solar energy.

The sites of deposition for the precursors of natural gas and oil were marine, whereas coal, and the associated methane, originates from terrestrial plants.

The common states in production of fossil fuels were (1) deposition of huge quantities of organic matter and of a comparitively small quantity of inorganic sediments; (2) anaerobic conditions that prevented oxidation of the organics to carbon dioxide; (3) increasing depth of burial which leads in temperature and pressure increase.

In this process the volume of the deposit is decreased and there is a loss of hydrogen, nitrogen and oxygen, which lead to the increased percentage of carbon; loss of recognisable plant remains; increase in hardness; decrease in volatile matter and increase in degree of aromatisation

The combustion of all fossil fuels release energy and produces carbon dioxide, water and nitrogen oxides, with sulphur dioxide in the case of coal and most oil (Eqn. 2.21).

$$\underset{\text{natural gas}}{CH_4} \text{ or } \underset{\text{coal and oil}}{C_2H_yS} + \underset{\text{air}}{O_2 + N_2} \longrightarrow H_2O + CO_2 + NO_x + SO_2 \quad (2.21)$$

2.17 Green House Effect

Atmospheric carbon-dioxide levels has been raised from about 290 ppm in 1860 to 310 ppm in 1980. At these concentrations carbon dioxide is not toxic and increased amounts in the atmosphere should increase rates of photosynthesis and plant growth. Earth's heat balance will be affected by increased amounts of atmospheric carbon dioxide as the molecules absorbs longer-wavelength, infra-red electromagnetic radiation, which is transparent to shorter-wavelength, visible and ultraviolet radiation. When the Earth reradiates the solar energy which has fallen on its surface the radiation is in the infra-red region of the spectrum. If the temperature of the radiation is lower than longer will be the wavelength of the maximum energy output. The lower the temperature of the radiation the longer the wavelength of the maximum-energy output. This means that the solar radiation is only partially absorbed by carbon dioxide on the 'way in' (Fig. 2.9), whereas a much higher proportion is absorbed on the 'way out' and is trapped in the atmosphere. As the concentration of carbon dioxide rises the amount of radiation trapped will also increase thereby the temperature of the atmosphere will rise. This phenomenon is called as greenhouse effect as the trapping principle is similar to that operating in a greenhouse, where the glass minimizes the loss of infra-red radiation. Now it is thought that the carbon-dioxide concentration will reach twice

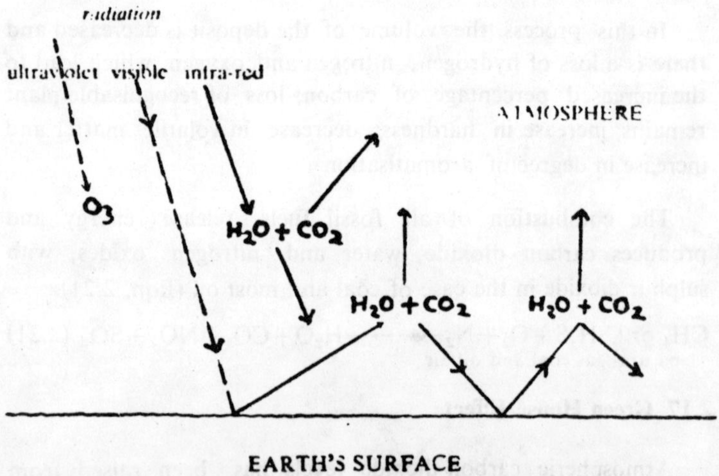

Fig. 2.9. The higher the concentration of water (H_2O) and carbon dioxide (CO_2), the greater the proportion of infra-red absorbed and then re-emitted to Earth rather then to space. The absorption of electromagnetic radiation by molecules in the Earth's atmosphere.

its pre-industrial level in 80-100 years' time and this will give a globally averaged temperature increase of about 2°C. Local temperature changes are expected to be larger (may be 5°C) at higher latitudes and less than this in the Tropics. Some regions will gain in food productivity whereas others will lose. It is apparent that the climatic changes will not appreciably decrease the productive capacity of the Earth, but it could well disturb the present imperfect economic and social balance of poor and wealthy nations.

It is thought that the emissions of carbon dioxide from fossil-fuel combustion are two or three times greater compared to emissions due to land-use changes such as forest clearing and burning. The land-use fig. are more unpredictable compare to the fossil-fuel figs. some people think that there may be an actual net removal of carbon dioxide from the atmosphere when reforestation and the abandonment of farmland which leads to the growth of scrub and trees) are taken into consideration. There is less carbon in normal agricultural crops than to the carbon which is bound up in bushe and trees occupying the same area.

The rate and magnitude of the carbon dioxide warming that could take place over the next century may be greater than any that have already taken place. The greenhouse effect is not simple phenomenon that has highlighted how little is known about the working of biogeochemical cycles and the consequences of their perturbation by human activities.

2.18 Ions and Radicals in the Atmosphere

One of the characteristics of the upper atmosphere which cannot be duplicated under laboratory conditions is the presence of significant levels of electrons and positive ions. Due to the rarefied conditions in the upper atmosphere, these ions may exist for long perions before recombining to form neutral species.

At altitudes of approximately 50 km and up, ions have been so prevalent that the region has been termed as the ionosphere. The presence of the ionsphere has been known since about 1901.

Ultraviolet light has been found to be the primary producer of ions in the ionsphere. In darkness when ultraviolet light no longer impinges on the ionosphere, the positive ions slowly recombine with free electrons. The process has been reported to be especially rapid in the lower regions of the ionsophere, where the concentration of species is relatively high. Thus the lower limit of the ionosphere lifts at night and makes possible the transmission of radio waves over much greater distances.

The earth's magnetic field is having a strong influence upon the ions in the upper atmosphere. Probably the best known manifestation of this phenomenon is found in the Van Allen belts discovered in 1958. These regions are having two belts of ionizing particles which circle the earth. If they are visualized as doughnuts, then the axis of the earth's magnetic field extencs through the holes in the doughnuts. In the inner belt the highly energetic ionizing radiation consists of protons. In the outer belt it consists of electrons. A schematic diagram of the Van Allen belts is shown in Fig. 2.10.

In addition to forming ions by photoionization, electromagnetic radiation in the upper atmosphere may produce free radicals :

$$CH_3-\overset{\overset{\displaystyle O}{\|}}{C}-H+h\nu=CH_3=HCO$$

Feee radicals are atoms, or groups of atoms with unpaired electrons. Most radicals are highly reactive. The upper atmosphere is so rarefied, however, that radicals may have half-lives of several minutes, or even longer. Radicals take part in chain reactions in which one of the products of each reaction is a radical. Eventually through processes such as reaction with another radical, one of the radicals in a chain is destroyed and the chain ends :

$$CH_3 + CH_3 = C_2H_6$$

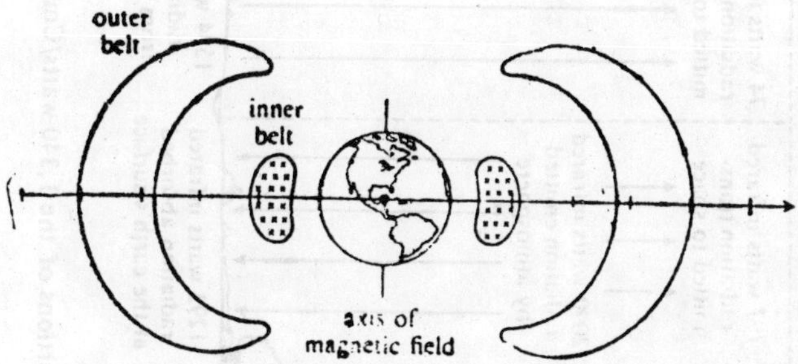

Fig. 2.10. Cross-section of Van Allen belts encircling the earth

This reaction is called a chain terminating reaction. Reactions involving free radicals are responsible for smog formation.

2.19 Particles in the Atmosphere

Particles constitute common and significant components of the atmosphere, especially the troposphere. Colloidal-sized particles in the atmosphere are called aerosols. Most aerosols from natural sources are having a diameter of less than 0.2 microns. These particles are termed as Aitken particles and are noted for their ability to induce formation of water droplets in supersaturated atmospheres. Aitken particles originate in nature from sea sprays, smokes, dusts, and the evaporation of organic materials from vegetation. Other typical particles of natural origin in the atmosphere include bacteria, fog, pollen grains, and volcanic ash.

Among the {atmospheric phenomena which involve aerosol particles have been electrification phenomena in the atmosphere, cloud formation, and fog formation. Particles help determine the heat balance of the earth's atmosphere by reflecting light.

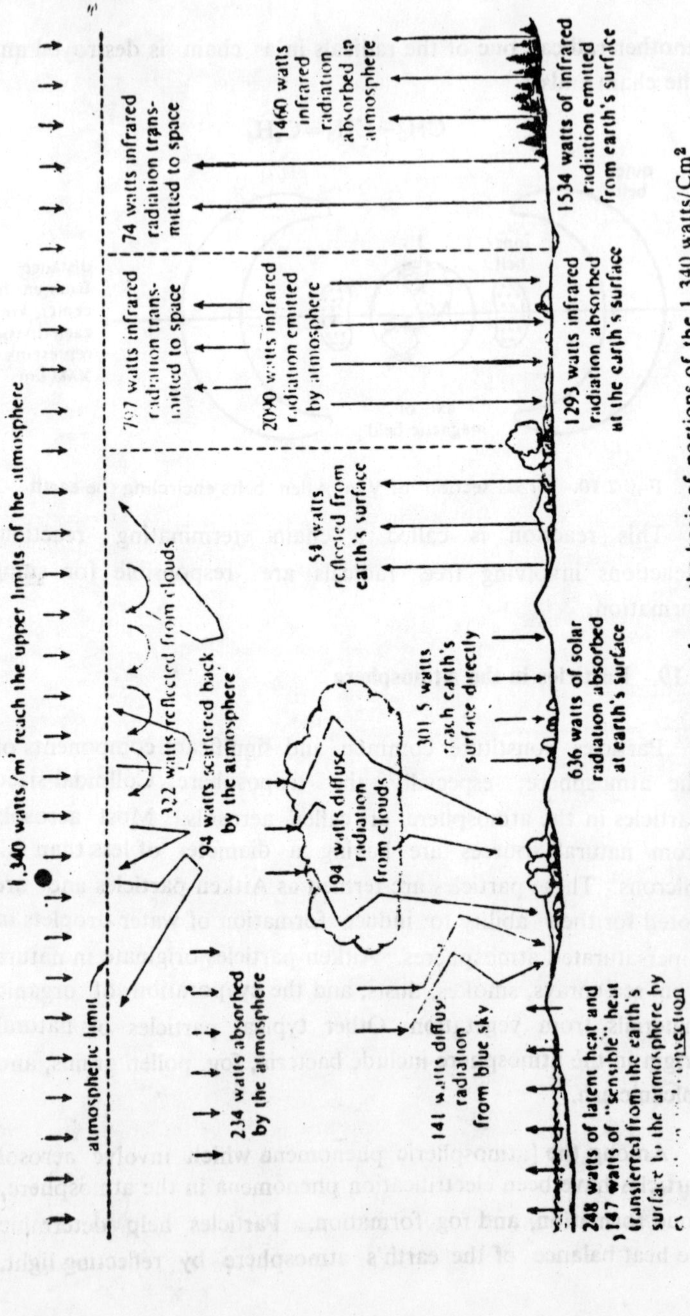

Fig. 2.11. Earth's radiation budget expressed on the basis of portions of the 1,340 watts/Cm² composing the solar flux

Probably the most important function of particles in the atmosphere has been their action as nuclei for the formation of ice crystals and water droplets. Current efforts at rain making are centered around the addition of condensing particles to atmospheres supersaturated with water vapor. Dry ice was used in early attempts; now silver iodide, which forms huge numbers of very small particles, is employed.

Particles are involved in many chemical reactions in the atmosphere. Neutralization reactions, which take place most readily in solution, may occur in water droplets suspended in the atmosphere. Small particles of metal oxides and carbon are having a catalytic effect on oxidation reactions. Particles may participate in oxidation reactions which are induced by light. It has been shown that zinc oxide surfaces, photosensitized by light, may cause the oxidation of water to hydrogen peroxide.

Particles may vary in number from several hundred per cubic centimetre in very pure air, to more than 10^5 per cubic centimetre, in highly polluted air. Their size lies in the range of $0.1-10\mu$. The particulate mass level has been found to vary from $10\mu g/m^3$ in clean air to $60-2000\ \mu g/m^3$ in the polluted air in urban areas.

In USA nearly 13.4 MT (metric tonnes) of primary particles have been given out per year, out of which about 5 MT have been smaller than 3μ.

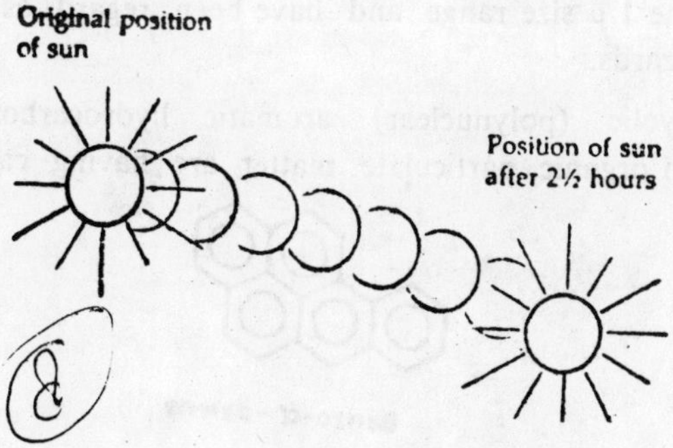

Metal oxides constitute a major group of inorganic particles in the atmosphere. They are originated from the combustion of fuels. Thus, particulate iron oxide is originated in the combustion of pyrite–containing cool :

$$3FeS_2 + 8O_2 \rightarrow Fe_3O_4 + 6\ SO_2$$

A part of the $CaCO_3$ in the ash fraction of coal charaged to CaO and gets discharged through the stack :

$$CaCO_3 + \text{heat} \rightarrow CaO + CO_2$$

Automobiles have been the main sources of lead particles in the atmosphere. Combustion of leaded gasoline releases lead halides through the exhaust system :

$$Pb(C_2H_5)_4 + O_2 + (\text{halogenated scavengers}) \rightarrow PbCl_2 + PbBr_2 + PbBrCl + CO_2 + H_2O$$

Aerosol mists are formed from sulphuric acid which are obtained by oxidation of sulphur dioxide which collects water vapour thereby forming small liquid droplets :

$$2SO_2 + O_3 + 2H_2O \rightarrow 2H_2SO_4$$

Organic particulate matter are formed from a wide veriety of sources such as emissions from vegetation and automobiles, combustion of fuel, etc. Typical organic particulate matter, which is obtained in the form of a benzene-extractable fraction from 200 air samples in USA reveals an average formula, C_{32}, H_{48} $O_{3\cdot8}$ $S_{0\cdot08}$, $\text{halogen}_{0\cdot065}$ alkoxy_{012}. Such particle have been in the 1 μ size range and have been regard as potential health hazards.

Polycyclic (polynuclear) aromatic hydrocarbons (PAH present in organic particulate matter are having carcinogenic

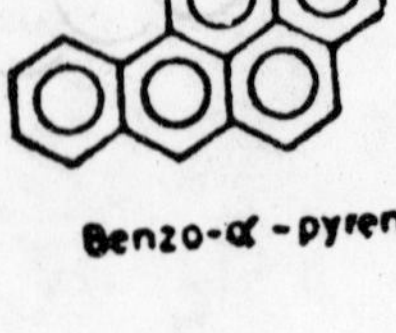

Benzo-α-pyrene

effect. Among these, benzo (α-) pyrene is a well characterised substance. PAH compounds commonly are found in urban atmospheres at about the 20 $\mu g/m^3$ level. They are obtained from the pyrolysis of higher paraffins present in fuels and plant material. High molecular weight paraffins are pyrolyzed for getting $C_{10}H_{22}$ which is further pyrolysed.

Most of the PAH compounds get adsorbed on soot particles.

Soot is obtained as a residue on combustion of fuel in power plants and automobiles. It constitutes nearly 50% of the particulates load in urban areas. Chemically, it refers to a highly condensed product of polynuclear aromatic hydrocarbons; having several thousand interconnected crystallites, *i.e.*, graphitic platelets each possessing nearly about 100 condensed aromatic rings. The hydrogen content of soot has been 1−3% and oxygen content about 5−10% due to partial surface oxidation. Due to its large surface area, soot is known to act as a carrier for toxic organics, *e.g.*, benzo (α) pyrene, and toxic trace metals, *e.g.*, beryllium, cadmium, chromium, manganese, nickel, vanadium, etc.

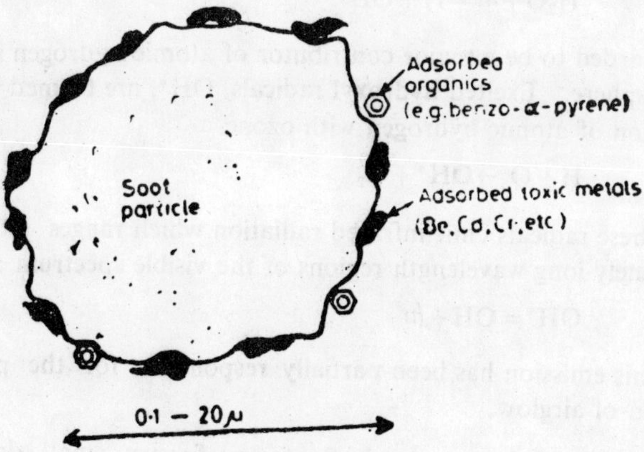

Fig. 2.12. Soot particle containing adsorbed toxic metals and organic carcinogens

In general, atmospheric particles enter the respiratory tract of human bodies. However, small particles (0.1-1μ size) reach the lungs and are retained there, bringing about health hazards. The removal of particulate matter from gas streams is regarded to be an important strategy for air pollution control, which will be described in a subsequent section.

2.20 Water in the Atmosphere

The water vapor content of the atmosphere has been found to very over a wide range, especially in the lower atmosphere. The normal range has been 1 to 3 per cent on a volume basis, although air may be having as little as 0.1 per cent of water and as much as 5 per cent. Water circulates through the atmosphere in the hydrologic cycle.

Water vapor absorbs infrared radiation, even more than does carbon dioxide, thereby determining the heat balance of the earth. Clouds formed from water vapor are able to reflect light from the sun and have a temperature lowering effect.

Gaseous water in the atmosphere in not known to participate appreciably in most atmospheric chemical reactions. However, photochemical reaction between water and ultraviolet light,

$$H_2O + h\nu = H + OH \qquad (2.1)$$

is regarded to be a major contributor of atomic hydrogen in the atmosphere. Excited hydroxyl radicals, OH*, are formed by the reaction of atomic hydrogen with ozone.

$$H + O_3 \rightarrow OH^* + O_2 \qquad (2.2)$$

These radicals emit infrared radiation which ranges into the extremely long wavelength regions of the visible spectrum :

$$OH^* = OH + h\nu \qquad (2.3)$$

This emission has been partially responsible for the phenomenon of airglow.

Condensed water vapor in the form of very small droplets has been of considerable significance in atmospheric chemistry.

Pollutant sulfur dioxide gets oxidized to sulfur trioxide in the atmosphere,

$$2SO_2 + O_2 = 2SO_3 \qquad (2.4)$$

and the sulfur trioxide gets incorporated into droplets of water,

$$SO_3 + H_2O = H_2SO_4 \qquad (2.5)$$

to form sulfuric acid. In some industrial areas the rainfall may have a remarkably low pH as a consequence. The harmful effects of some air pollutants – for instance, the corrosion of metals by acid forming gases – requires the presence of water which may come from the atmosphere. The presence of water vapor has an important influence upon pollution-induced fog formation under some circumstances. Water vapor interacting with particulate matter in the atmosphere may reduce visibility to undesirable levels through the formation of aerosol particles.

2.21 Sulfur Cycle

Sulfur which is an essential element in protein synthesis, provides linkage between polypeptide chains in protein molecules. As it is known that the life on earth could not exists without sulfur. It is less likely, however, to be limiting of ecosystem productivity than phosphours. In nature, sulfur is found in elemental form and in different oxidation states, including hydrogen sulfide (H_2S), sulfides (SO_2), and sulfates (SO_4). Organic sulfur in plants and animals is decomposed to H_2S by bacterial action, and the H_2S is oxidized further to sulfates such as $(NH_4)_2SO_4$ by sulfur-oxidizing bacteria (Fig. 2.13). These sulfates are then taken up by plants as primary nutrients. Hydrogen sulfide from time to time can accumulate by rapid protein breakdown. Below 150 meters in block rea the concentrations of H_2S and H_2SO_4 are so large as to exclude all forms of life other than sulfur bacteria. In polluted estuaries, large accumulations of algal sea lettuce can undergo primary decomposition to give obnoxious quantities of H_2S. In some coastal areas, it has been known to be sufficiently severe to cause paint blistering on nearby houses. Sulfur is also locked into coal and petroleum and when these products are burned it is released as sulfur dioxide.

These discussions explains the cyclic flow of essential elements between the living and nonliving organisms of the ecosystems.

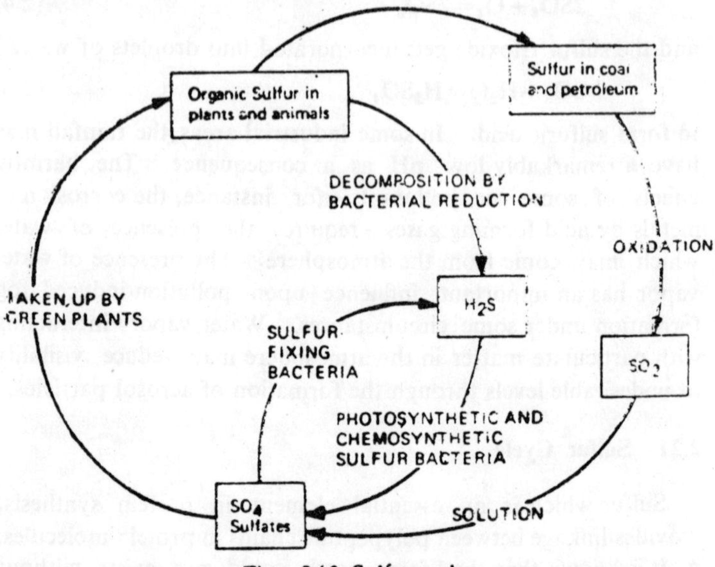

Fig. 2.13. Sulfur cycle

Similar flow-diagrams can be made for all the other elements which play a vital role in living systems, like iron, magnesium, sodium, potassium, manganese, cobalt, and several others. Our known how of all of these cycles serves to put the stress on the interrelations of the living and nonliving world, and to show us that the biosphere is a not a simple biochemical system which depends on the proper functioning of many organisms.

2.22 Micro-organisms and the sulphur cycle

Micro-organisms influence sulphur biogeochemical cycling. Sulphur tends to be present in living organisms in its most reduced form, sulphur (−2) as hydrosulphide group. This sulphur has the ability to form sulphur-sulphur bonds which allows cross-linking in proteins, so-called disulphide linkages. There can be two types of bonding first inter-molecular bonding linking together adjacent proteins and so developing large-scale structures (*e.g.* hair and nails) and second intra-molecular bonding, giving specific spatial characteristics to the protein (*e.g.* enzymes). When organic sulphur compounds are decomposed with the help of bacteria, the initial excreted sulphur product is generally hydrogen sulphide.

With the help of dioxygen the oxidation of the reduced forms of sulphur may occur (Equ. 2.22) either through the action of micro-organisms in the soil, the sediment and the water column, or without biological control, specially in the atmosphere.

$$\underset{\text{hydrogen sulphide}}{HS} \dashrightarrow \underset{\text{(sulphur : may not be formed)}}{(S)} \xrightarrow{O_2} \underset{\text{sulphur dioxide}}{SO_2} \xrightarrow{O_2} \underset{\text{sulphur trioxide}}{SO_3} \longrightarrow \underset{\text{sulphate}}{SO_4^{2-}} \quad (2.22)$$

The micro-organism combines it with a half-reaction such as the oxidation of carbohydrate that will give an overall negative free-energy change, giving rise to sulphate reduction (Eqn. 2.23).

$$SO_4^{2-} + H^+ + 2CH_2O \rightarrow HS^- + 2H_2O + 2CO_2 \; \Delta G, -25.6 \text{ kJ mol}^{-1}e^- \quad (2.23)$$

The sulphate' which act as an electron acceptor and the oxidation of the carbohydrate can proceed. The energy released to the organism is only about one-fifth of that which is can be obtained when dioxygen acts as the electron acceptor in aerobic respiration.

The results of this order of energy production is that if all four mechanisms are possible, then organisms which gain their energy by aerobic respiration will be favoured. The large quantity of [energy the aerobic respirators obtain from a given carbohydrate source will allow them to develop at the expense of micro-organisms depending upon less efficient energy-releasing processes. When the dioxygen supply becomes depleted and the conditions become anaerobic, the nitrate reducers will be most favoured. The nitrate concentration is much lower companed to the sulphate concentration under marine conditions and the nitrate is soon depleted, which allows the sulphate-reducing micro organisms to become dominant. The formation of hydrogen sulphide (H_2S) is a characteristic feature of anaerobic marine sediments due to the high levels of sulphate, than nitrate, in sea water. Iron, is present in relatively greater quantities, forms the major sulphide mineral reservoir as troilite, FeS (Eqn. 2.24), and as iron pyrites, FeS_2 (Equ. 2.25)

$$\underset{\text{iron(III) hydroxide}}{2Fe(OH)_3} + 3H_2S \dashrightarrow \underset{\text{troilite}}{2FeS} + S + 6H_2O \qquad (2.24)$$

$$FeS + S \dashrightarrow \underset{\text{pyrites}}{FeS_2} \qquad (2.25)$$

The black colour of several sediments is partially because of the presence of iron sulphides as well as organic matter. The association of sulphide minerals, specially iron pyrites, with rich organic marine sedimentary deposits like black shales and coal can lead to acidity when these deposits are exposed to the atmosphere of the earth. Such exposure can be because of the uplift and weathering or mining. Oxidation of the sulphides leads to the formation of sulphuric acid (Eqn. 2.26).

$$\underset{\text{pyrites}}{2FeS_2} + 2H_2O + O_2 \dashrightarrow \underset{\text{iron (II) sulphate}}{2FeSO_4} + \underset{\text{sulphuric acid}}{2H_2SO_4} \qquad (2.26)$$

This redox reaction can take place rapidly in the presence of water and dioxygen, particularly when micro-organisms are involved. The acid produced may be neutralised as it passes through rocks and soil in the ground water if it is produced slowly by natural weathering processes. Due to greater solubility of many metals in acid solutions, extensive leaching occurs. Several black shales contain high concentrations of potentially toxic elements and the increased mobilisation of these metals in the acidic waters may cause elevated levels to appear in plants and aquatic biota. The problems becomes more serious in metalliferous mine-waste dumps which can have some toxic metals present in parts per hundred, rather than the parts per million of normal rocks and soils. The mining of metal-sulphide ores and coal leads to the exposure of large quantities of sulphides and therefore to the production of much greater quantities of acid in localised areas than does the weathering of shales. The resultant large addition of acid, sometimes enriched in toxic metals, can lead to major pollution problems in the areas surrounding the mining operation.

2.23 Chemical and Photochemical Reactions in the Atmosphere

One of the primary obstacles encountered in studying atmospheric chemistry is that the chemist generally must deal with incredibly low concentrations. The detection and analysis of reaction products is quite difficult. Simulating high altitude conditions in the laboratory can be extremely hard due to interferences, such as those from species given off from container walls under conditions of very low pressure. Many chemical reactions which need a third body to absorb excess energy occur very slowly in the upper atmosphere where there is a sparse concentration of third bodies, but take place readily in a container whose wall effectively absorbs energy. Container walls may serve as catalysts for some important reactions, or they may absorb important species and react chemically with the more reactive ones.

The absorption of light by chemical species can cause reactions which do not otherwise take place under the conditions (particularly the temperature) of the medium in the absence of light. Thus photochemical reactions, even in the absence of a chemical catalyst, take place at temperatures much lower than those which otherwise would be required. Such photochemical reactions, induced by intense solar radiation, play a very important role in ascertaining the nature and ultimate fate of a chemical species in the atmosphere.

Electronically excited molecules have been one of three relatively reactive and unstable species which are encountered in the atmosphere and which are strongly involved with atmospheric chemical processes. The other two species are atoms or molecular fragments with unshared electrons, called free radicals, and ionized atoms or molecular fragments.

Electronically excited molecules are produced when stable molecules absorb energetic electromagnetic radiation in the ultra-violet or visible region of the spectrum. A molecule may possess several possible excited states, but generally ultraviolet and visible radiation are energetic enough to excite molecules only to several of the lowest energy levels. The nature of the excited state may be understood considering the disposition of electrons in a molecule. Most molecules have an even number of electrons. The electrons occupy orbitals, with a maximum of two electrons having opposi.e spin occupying the same orbital. The absorption of light may promote one of these electrons to a vacant orbital of higher energy. If the electron thus promoted is still of opposite spin from its former partner, the excited state is called a singlet state, and if the electron spins are the same, the excited state is called a triplet state :

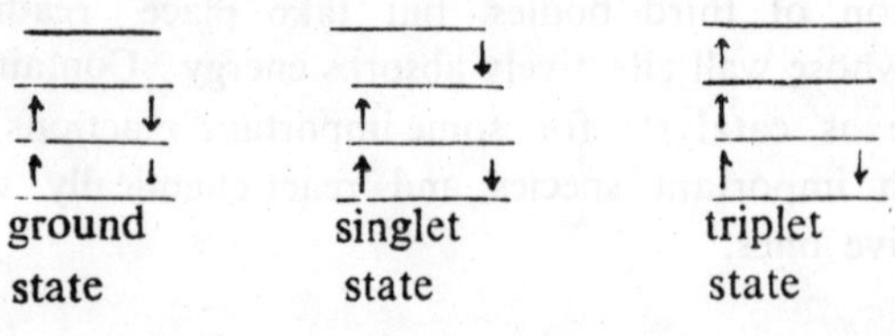

These excited states are energized compared to the ground state and are chemically reactive species. Later their participation in atmospheric chemical reactions, such as those involved in smog formation, will be described in detail.

Two conditions must be met before a photochemical reaction will occur. The first of these laws of photochemistry is that light must be absorbed by the reacting species. If the absorbed light is in the visible region of the sun's spectrum, the absorbing species is colored. Colored NO_2 is the prime example of such a species in the atmosphere. The second law of photochemistry is that the primary photochemical process involves activation of the molecule by the absorption of one quantum of light. The energy of one quantum is equal to the product $h\nu$, where h is Planck's constant, 6.62×10^{-27} erg sec, and ν is the frequency of the absorbed light, sec^{-1}.

An intermolecular energy transfer may take place in which an excited species transfers energy to another species. A subsequent reaction by the second molecule is termed as a photosensitized reaction. It is believed that part of airglow arises from luminescence by excited sodium atoms, Na*, formed in the atmosphere by an intermolecular energy transfer involving the following reaction :

$$O_2^* + Na \rightarrow O_2 + Na^*$$

In some cases only energy transfer within the molecule occurs,

$$XY^* = XY^\dagger$$

a process called intramolecular transfer, where the dagger, †, denotes an excited state different from the initial one. Finally, the excited species may undergo spontaneous isomerization,

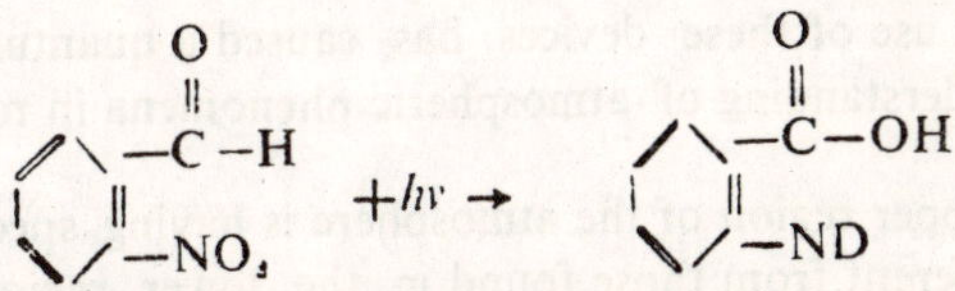

as in the conversion of O-nitrobenzaldehyde to O-nitrosobenzoic acid, a reaction used in chemical actinometers to measure exposure to electromagnetic radiation.

The absorption of very energetic radiation may result in the detachment of an electron,

$$N_2 + h\nu = N_2^+ + e$$

a process called photoionization. Photoionization often is considered a subcategory of photodissociation in which one of the dissociation products is an electron.

Light absorbed in the infrared region is not sufficiently energetic to break chemical bonds. The receptor molecules gain vibrational and rotational energy. The energy absorbed as infrared radiation ultimately is dissipated as heat and raises the temperature of the atmosphere. The absorption of infrared radiation is very important in the earth's acquiring heat from the sun and in the retention of energy radiated from the earth's surface.

2.24 Major Regions of the Atmosphere

The science of planetary atmospheres is termed as aeronomy. In addition to dealing with the chemical composition and reactions of these atmospheres, it involves their movement and thermal balance. In order to understand atmospheric chemistry it becomes essential first to have some understanding of the physical characteristics of the atmosphere.

It is possible to divide the atmosphere into a number of different regions depending upon the system of classification. The most general classification has been that of the lower atmosphere (up to approximately 50 km) and the upper atmosphere. Until the development of high altitude rockets and earth satellites, only the lower atmosphere was accessible for study. However, use of these devices has caused a quantum jump of man's understanding of atmospheric phenomena in recent years.

The upper region of the atmosphere is having species appreciably different from those found in the lower region. As the lower regions are relatively homogeneous in composition, one system of classification divides the atmosphere into regions called the homosphere (having little variation in composition) and the heterosphere (having a high variation in composition.)

The system most commonly used today (1975) is able to divide the atmosphere upon the basis of temperature changes. These temperature regions and their characteristics have been summarized in Table 2.2 and have been depicted schematically in Fig. 2.14. In addition to the regions listed, a fifth region, the exosphere, is sometimes defined. Some of the species in the exosphere attain sufficient kinetic energy to break loose from the gravitational field of the earth and go into outer space.

The boundaries of the troposphere have been found to be influenced by a number of factors, including temperature and the nature of the underlying terrestrial surface. Even during a one-day period the upper limit of the troposphere has been found to vary by a kilometer or more. The troposphere has been characterized by falling temperature with increasing altitude, as the distance from the heat-radiating earth increases.

Table 2.2

Major Regions of the Atmosphere and Their Characteristics

Region	*Temperature range, °C**	*Altitude range, km**	*Significant chemical species*
troposphere	15 to—56	0 to 11	N_2, O_2, CO_2, H_2O
stratosphere	—56 to—2	11 to 50	O_3
mesosphere	— 2 to—92	50 to 85	O_2^+, NO^+
thermosphere	—92 to 1200	85 to 500	O_2^+, O^+, NO^+

*These figures are values ranging from the lowest part of the region to the highest part. They may vary.

In the absence of air pollution the composition of the troposphere has been somewhat homogenous. This homogeneity has been due largely to mixing by the constantly circulating air masses in the troposphere. The water content of the troposphere, however, is extremely variable due to cloud formation, precipitation, and evaporation of water from terrestrial water bodies.

Troposphere. The zone nearest the earth, the troposphere, is named from the Greek tropein (to turn, to rotate, to change). One property that changes in the troposphere is the temperature. It drops to—55°C (—65°F) by the time an altitude of about 16-18 km (10-11 miles) is reached. The rate of temperature drop is about 6.4°C per 1000 metres (3.5°F per 1000 feet), a figure called the normal environmental lapse rate. The region through which this lapse rate occurs defines the troposphere. At the aquator the troposphere is about 18 kilometres (11 miles) thick, but at the poles it is only about 8 kilometres (5 miles) thick. Essentially all the atmosphere's water vapor is in the troposphere which therefore encloses essentially all the storms and precipitation of the earth. The jet stream occurs at an altitude of 10.5-12 kilometres (35,000—40,000 feet; 6.5—7.5 miles).

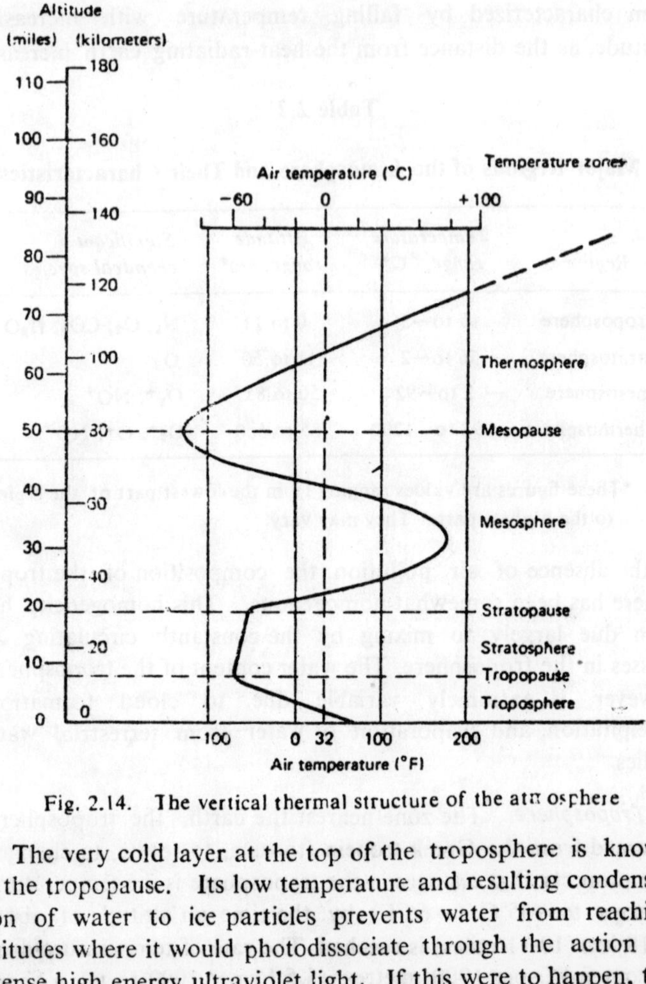

Fig. 2.14. The vertical thermal structure of the atmosphere

The very cold layer at the top of the troposphere is known as the tropopause. Its low temperature and resulting condensation of water to ice particles prevents water from reaching altitudes where it would photodissociate through the action of intense high energy ultraviolet light. If this were to happen, the hydrogen produced would escape the earth's atmosphere (this happened to much of the hydrogen and helium originally present in the earth's atmosphere). Hence the tropopause acts as a barrier preventing the net loss of hydrogen from the earth with accompanying decomposition of wate.

The troposphere has been the region in which we live and is the region to which this book is primarily devoted.

The weather patterns that we are familiar with are all contained within the troposphere, and mixing in the region is fast, of the order of weeks within a hemisphere, and of 1 to 2 years between hemispheres. Vertical mixing occurs in the troposphere but movement into the stratosphere is inhibited by the temperature inversion.

Stratosphere. This zone starts at the top of the troposphere, at a thin atmospheric "shell" called the tropopause, where the temperature begins to stay fairly constant, increasing slightly, in going to an altitude of 50 kilometres (31 miles). The stratosphere includes much of the ozone layer. The warming trend in the stratosphere is caused by a cycle of chemical changes in the ozone layer which converts all the incoming high energy ultraviolet rays to heat (see Ozone). If these rays reached the earth's surface, life as we know it would be impossible. The stratopause marks the narrow zone at the top of the stratosphere where the temperature begins to fall again with increasing altitude as the mesosphere is entered.

The stratosphere is characterized by a rising temperature as the altitude increases. The temperature reaches a maximum at the upper limit of the stratosphere. The temperature increase of the stratosphere is due to the presence of ozone, which may reach a level of 10 ppm by volume in the mid-region of the stratosphere. Ozone absorbs energy in the form of ultraviolet light and causes an increase in temperature.

The stratosphere has been of interest to aeronautical scientists because it is traversed by airplanes; to communication scientists because of radio and television communications; and to air pollution scientists because global transport of pollution, particularly the debris of above ground atomic bomb tests and of volcanic eruptions, occurs in the stratosphere; and because absorption and scattering of solar energy also occurs in the stratosphere.

The principal chemical species in the stratosphere. N_2, O_2, O_3 and some H_2O, are chemically active because of their interaction with ultraviolet solar radiation.

The interaction of a species with radiation, producing chemical changes, is photochemistry. Radiation is absorbed forming an activated species and, provided the conditions are suitable, a new species is formed.

Though most of the energetic radiation from the sun has been filtered out at higher altitudes, some important chemical reactions take place in the troposphere, particularly at the atmosphere/biosphere and atmosphere/lithosphere interfaces. Two of these reactions are photosynthesis, the overall process given by the two equations :

Fig. 2.15. The variation in the concentrations of N_2, O_2, H_2O and O_3 with height. Source : M.J. McEwad and L.F. Phillips, Chemistry of the Atmosphere, Edwarn Arnold, London (1975)

$$2H_2O \rightarrow O_2 + 4H^+ + 4e^- \quad (2.27)$$

$$CO_2 + 4H^+ + 4e^- \rightarrow [CH_2O] + H_2O \quad (2.28)$$

and nitrogen fixation :

$$N_2 \xrightarrow[\text{hydrogenase}]{\text{nitrogenase}} NH_3 \rightarrow \underset{\text{in the soil}}{NO_2^- \rightarrow NO_3^-} \quad (2.29)$$

Chemical reactions, for example, hydrolysis and oxidation, also occur at the surface of the earth (weathering, see later). The corrosion of iron is represented by the equation :

$$Fe-2e \rightarrow Fe^{2+} \quad (2.30)$$

$$O_2+2H_2O+4e \rightarrow 4OH^- \quad (2.31)$$

i.e. $$2Fe+O_2+2H_2O \rightarrow 2Fe^{2+}+4OH^- \xrightarrow[\text{air}]{\text{in}} \underset{\text{rust}}{Fe_2O_3 \times H_2O} \quad (2.32)$$

Electrical discharges in the atmosphere initiate reaction between nitrogen and oxygen as follows :

$$N_2+O_2 \xrightarrow{h\nu} 2NO \xrightarrow{O_3} 2NO_2 \quad (2.33)$$

The far ultraviolet radiation (wavelength$<$190 nm) is removed before it reaches the stratospher by atomic nitrogen and oxygen. A considerable portion of longer wavelength ultraviolet, (*i.e.*, below 340 nm) is removed in the stratosphere, for example, radiation of wavelength$<$242 nm promotes the reaction :

$$O_2+h\nu \rightarrow O+O^*. \quad (2.34)$$

The atomic oxygen produced reacts with O_2 to form ozone :

$$O^*+O_2+M \rightarrow O_3+M^*, \quad (2.35)$$

and the ozone absorbs ultraviolet radiation of wevelength

$$O_3+h\nu \rightarrow O_2+O, \quad (2.36)$$

$<$340 nm; followed by the reaction;

$$O_3+O \rightarrow 2O_2. \quad (2.37)$$

Hence a cycle of ozone formation and destruction (Chapman mechanism) exits,

i.e., $$3O_2 \rightarrow 2O_3, \quad (2.38)$$

and $$2O_3 \rightarrow 3O_2. \quad (2.39)$$

Other reactions can also occur, the principal among which is the reaction of ozone with nitric oxide.

$$NO+O_3 \rightarrow NO_2+O_2 \quad (2.40)$$

$$NO_2+O \rightarrow NO+O_2 \quad (2.41)$$

$$NO_2+h\nu \rightarrow NO+O \; (\lambda<400 \text{ nm}). \quad (2.42)$$

The overall process may be put as before;

$$2O_3 \rightarrow 3O_2 \text{ [twice reaction (2.40) plus reactions (2.41) and (2.42)]} \quad ...(2.43)$$

and accounts for removal of approximately 70% ozone. Species HO_x are involved in similar reactions.

The absorption of ultraviolet radiation in the stratosphere prevents virtually all radiation below 290 nm, and most between 290 and 320 nm, from reaching the earth (Fig. 2.36) Present day biological life has been protected from this radiation, a situation that may not continue as gaseous pollutants are added to the atmosphere.

In reaction (2.35) an excited species, M*, is producted. The energy may be transferred as heat, which would explain the rise in temperature within the stratosphere. Infrared radiation also absorbed and re-emitted by ozone adds to the temperature rise.

Mesophere. The mesosphere, on top of the stratosphere, extends roughly to 80 kilometres (50 miles), and its temperature drops to between −80 and −90°C at the mesopause, a

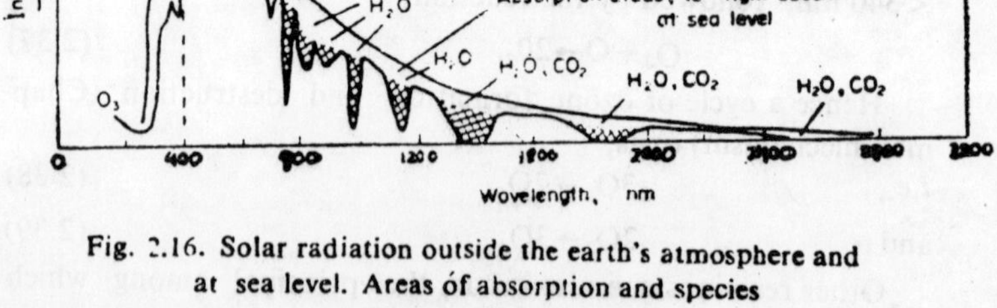

Fig. 2.16. Solar radiation outside the earth's atmosphere and at sea level. Areas of absorption and species contributing are indicated

thin zone where the temperature stabilizes and soon starts to rise again as the thermosphere is ascended.

The principal chemical species in the mesosphere are N_2, O_2, O_2^+ and NO^+, and in the thermosphere are N_2, O_2, O_2^+, O, O^+ and NO^+. The thermosphere is also called the ionosphere as ionization of molecular and atomic species takes place in the lower layers. These layers are responsible for the reflection of radio-waves.

Thermosphere. This zone is above 80 kilometres (50 miles) altitude. The temperature becomes very high, but the air has such a low density that it can hold very little heat. Any denser object in the thermosphere will be extremely hot in sunlight but very cold at night.

The temperature falls with increasing altitude in the mesosphere due to a decrease in the levels of the radiation—absorbing species, particularly ozone. In the higher altitudes of the mesosphere and above, molecules and atoms can completely escape the earth's atmosphere. (This region is called the exosphere). The temperature rises to a maximum of approximately 1200°C in the thermosphere due to the absorption of highly energetic radiation of wavelengths less than approximately 200 nm by species in this region.

Atmospheric pressure tends to decrease as an approximately exponential function of altitude. Ideally, in the absence of mixing and at a constant absolute temperature, T, the pressure at any given height, P_h, is given by the expontential equation.

$$P_h = P_0 e^{-Mgh/RT} \qquad (2.44)$$

where P_0 refers to the pressure at zero altitude (sea level), M the average gram molecular weight of air (28.97 grams/mole), g the acceleration of gravity (981 cm sec^{-2} at sea level), *h* the altitude in cm, and R the gas constant (8.314×10^7 erg deg^{-1} $mole^{-1}$). For consistency the units in Equation (2.44) are given in the c.g.s. system, although height is normally measured in metres or kilometres and it becomes necessary in using Equation (2.44) to convert height to cm by multiplying by the appropriate factors.

The pressure drops by the factors e^{-1} for each increase in altitude equal to the scale height, defined as RT/Mg. At an average sea level temperature of 288°K the scale height is 8×10^5 cm or 8 km. At an attitude of 8 km the pressure is only about 39% of sea level pressure.

In order to get a better picture of the variation of pressure with altitude, Equation (2.44) may be converted to the logarithmic (base 10) form and h expressed in kilometres :

$$\log P_h = \log P_0 - \frac{Mgh \times 10^5}{2.303KT} \qquad (2.45)$$

If the pressure is taken as 1.00 atm at sea level, the equation becomes simply :

$$\log P_h = -\frac{Mgh \times 10^5}{2.303RT} \qquad (2.46)$$

Starting with a sea level pressure of 1.00 atm and assuming a constant temperature of 373°K (0°C), Fig. 2.17 depicts the variation of pressure with altitude from 0 to 100 km.

Actual atmospheric pressure deviates from the ideal shown in Fig. 2.17 because of mixing of air masses and non-uniform temperature distribution with altitude. The actual pressure tends to be somewhat higher than that shown in Fig. 2.17 at altitude up to 15 km and somewhat lower at altitudes above 15 km. Note also that the pressure decreases by a factor of 10 for each approximately 20 km increase in altitude.

In terms of bulk, by far the greatest portion of the atmosphere is confined to the region very close to the surface of the earth. Less than 1% of atmospheric gases are more than 40 km from the earth's surface. Such an altitude is of course miniscule compared to the radius of the earth.

The zones just discussed may be defined by changes of temperature with altitude. Changes in chemical composition or activity also occur with altitude. Up to about 80 kilometres (50 miles) the proportions of components remain nearly constant, and the long zone up to that altitude is sometimes called the homosphere. Within it is a region called the chemosphere extending from the upper troposphere where a huge number

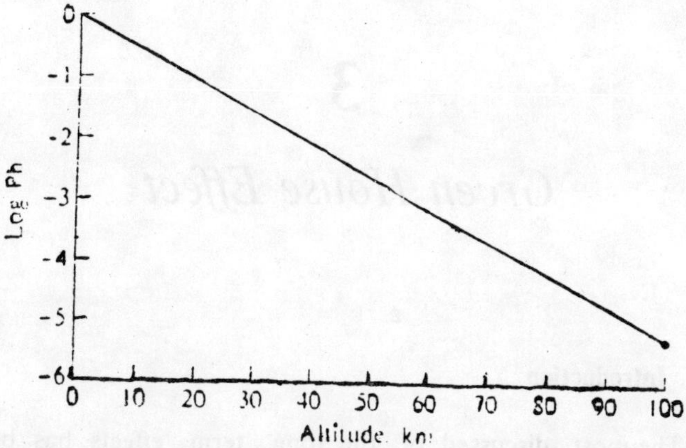

Fig. 2.17 Variation of atmospheric pressure with altitude assuming idealized conditions at 273°K.

of chemical changes occur powered by solar radiation. Ozone production is one such activity. Above the homosphere lies the heterosphere. For its first 40 kilometres (25 miles), the ionosphere, the very thin concentration of atoms and molecules, exists largely as electrically charged particles called ions. This globe-enveloping band of ions reflects outgoing radio waves back to earth, making radio transmission possible well beyond the horizon. Television waves are not reflected, and a TV transmitter's range does not extent beyond the horizon Meteorites entering the earth's atmosphere generally out in the ionosphere.

3

Green House Effect

3.1. Introduction

The most discussed of the long term effects has been the changing concentration of carbon dioxide. This has been carefully measured at Mauna Loa in the Hawaian Islands for more than a decade. Seasonal variations have been seen as well as a gradual increase on the average value of some 0.7 ppm each year, to reach a present value of about 320 ppm. The

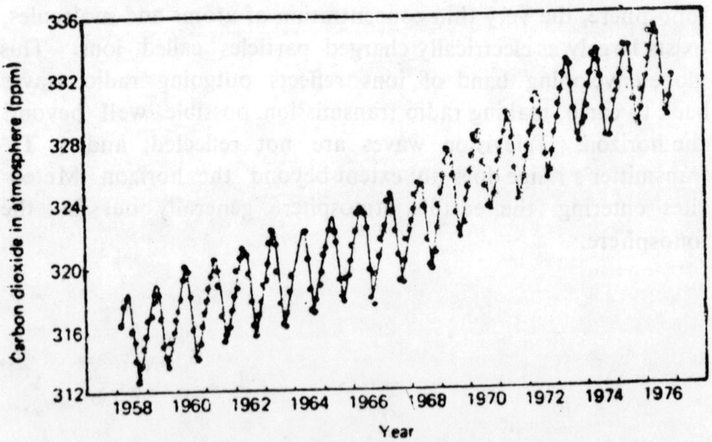

Fig. 3.1. The trend in carbon dioxide concentration in the Mauna Loa Observatory [Taken from the results of Charles D. Keeling reproduced in Scientific American, 238,37 (1978).]

seasonal variation can be explained by the greater demand forc arbon dioxide by plants during the spring and summer when they are growing rapidly, decreasing the amount in the atmosphere. Records of carbon dioxide concentrations over the last century have revealed that there has been occurring a gradual increase from about 290 ppm before 1890 to the present value (Fig. 3.1).

Measurements at Mauna Loa, Hawaii, an area away from heavy industrial concentrations, indicate a yearly increase of approximately 0.7 ppm (during 1958.65) and 0.5 ppm from 1965. An average increase of 0.6 ppm Yr^{-1} (0.2% Yr^{-}) approximates to the amount of CO_2 formed from the burning of fossil fuels. Regular seasonal variations in the concentration of CO_2 correlates with photosynthetic activity, and in the Northern Hemisphere, the concentration peaks around April, and is lowest around September-October. It is believed that the major contribution to the seasonal variation is the photosynthetic activity of mid latitude forests. Forest destruction could have a serious affect on the levels of atmospheric CO_2. Carbon dioxide undergoes photochemical reactions, producing CO at higher altitudes in the atmosphere.

$$CO_2 + \underset{(uv)}{h\nu} \rightarrow CO + O \tag{3.1}$$

This is a significant source of CO at these levels.

The world's climate is dependent on the global heat balance, a mean temperature change of 2-3K would have a marked effect. Of the 8.4×10^4 Jm^{-2} min^{-1} (1400 watt m^{-2}) energy that enters the earth's atmosphere, approximately 47% reaches the earth's surface and adjacent atmosphere, directly or after being scattered. The incoming ultraviolet, visible and infrared energy has a max intensity, at the earth's surface around 483 nm, while energy re-emitted from the earth is only in the infrared region (2000.40,000 nm) with a maximum intensity around 10,000 nm. If this energy was lost to the atmosphere the temperature of the earth's surface would be around $-20°$ to $-40°C$. However, some of the infrared is absorbed by water vapour and carbon dioxide in the air and re-emitted in all directions, some of which returns to the earth producing an average temperature of around 14°C.

Water has three fundamental vibration modes, ν_1, ν_2 and ν_3 (Table 3.1), while CO_2 has four modes, ν_1, ν_{2a}, ν_{2b} and ν_3 (modes ν_{2a} and ν_{2b} are degenerate). The strong infrared absorptions due to water occur below 8000 nm (and >20,000 nm) while the ν_2 absorption of CO_2 is the most intense and absorbs over the region 13,000—18,000 nm. This leaves an infrared exit window between 8000 – 13,000 nm.

The earth's mean temperature rose 0.4°C from 1880 to 1940, and from 1945 has dropped around 0.1°C. The initial rise has been correlated with an increase in atmospheric concentration of CO_2 (Fig. 3.1).

Table 3.1

Vibrational Modes of H_2O vapour and CO_2

	Normal Modes	*Symbol*	*Wavelength nm*
H_2O	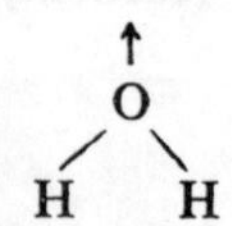	ν_1	2,730
	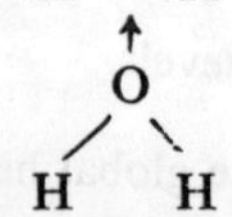	ν_2	6,300
	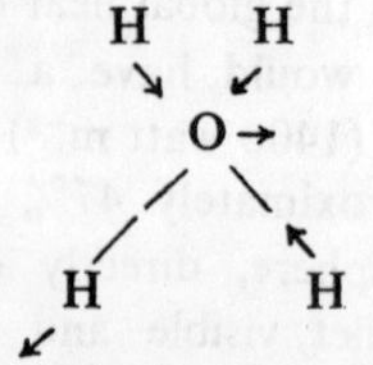	ν_3	2,660
CO_2	←O–C–O→	ν_1	7,400
	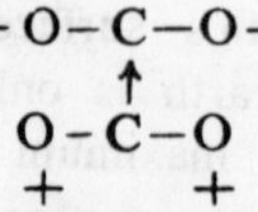	ν_{2a}	
	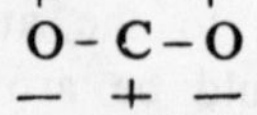	ν_{2b}	15,000
	←O - C →←O	ν_3	4,300

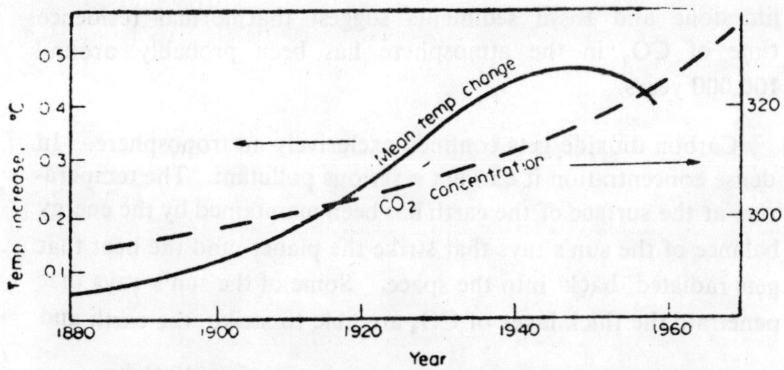

Fig. 3.2. Changes in mean world temperature and CO_2 levels in the atmosphere

A large amount of carbon dioxide gets introduced into the atmosphere from fossil fuel burning, furnaces and breathing of animals. From fossil fuel alone, more than $2.5 \times 10_{13}$ tonnes of CO_2 is being emitted into the atmosphere each year. Not all of the CO_2 injected into the atmosphere remains there; about half of if gets utilized by plant life or absorbed by water of the oceans. Part of the CO_2 dissolved in the ocean may get precipitated or incorporated in marine organisms. In this respect aquatic plants in the ocean are playing an important role in maintaining CO_2 equilibrium between the atmosphere and the surface layers of the ocean (up to 100 metres deep). Part of the CO_2 taken up by terrestrial plants gets deposited in dead vegetation and humus on the forest floor. Some of it, in the form of organic plant parts, has been eaten by herbivorous animals and gets deposited on or in the soil. However, much of CO_2 is still left in the atmosphere. An increase in atmospheric carbon dioxide will influence the photosynthesis, and consequently on plant growth by its direct fertilising effect, especially in hot tropical environments and a longer growing season in temperate regions. This potential fertilising effect should be exploitable by using modified crop varieties and agriculture practices to compensate for the disadvantageous effects of temperature increase. Carbon dioxide emitted by volcanoes during several billion years was at least 40,000 times that still present in the air. On a global time scale, the known amounts of CO_2 in limestone and fossil sediments suggest that normal residence time of CO_2 in the atmosphere has been probably around 100,000 years.

Carbon dioxide gets confined exclusively to troposphere. In dense concentration it can act a serious pollutant. The temperature at the surface of the earth has been maintained by the energy balance of the sun's rays that strike the planet and the heat that gets radiated back into the space. Some of the sun's rays that penetrate the thick layer of CO_2 are able to strike the earth and

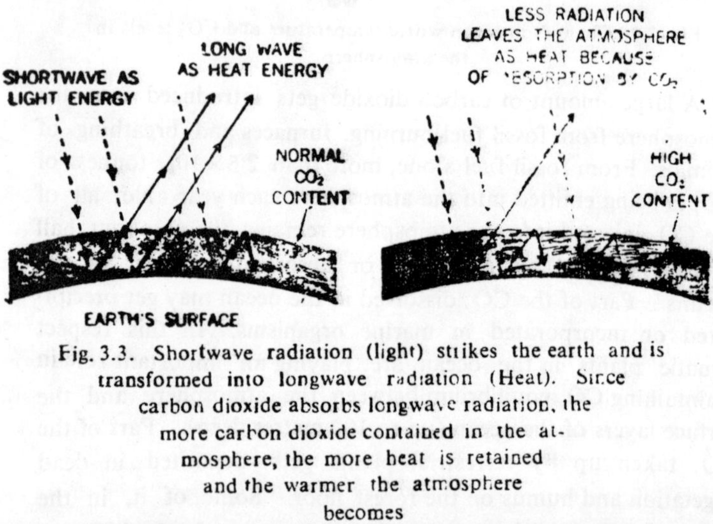

Fig. 3.3. Shortwave radiation (light) strikes the earth and is transformed into longwave radiation (Heat). Since carbon dioxide absorbs longwave radiation, the more carbon dioxide contained in the atmosphere, the more heat is retained and the warmer the atmosphere becomes

get converted into heat. The heated earth is able to reradiate this absorbed energy as radiations of longer wavelengths. Much of this does not pass through CO_2 layer to outer space but gets absorbed by the CO_2 and water in the atmosphere and adds to the heat that has been already present. Thus the earth's atmosphere heats up (Fig. 3.3). This phenomenon is termed as the green house effect. Carbon dioxide thus acts like the glass of a green house and on a global scale, tends to warm the air in the lower levels of the atmosphere.

In the "greenhouse effect", increase in the CO_2 concentration means more infrared radiation is trapped and re-emitted back to the earth (Fig. 3.4), producing a build up of infrared radiation in the atmosphere and a mean global temperature rise. Estimates of the rise in temperature with increasing CO_2 concentration range from 0.1 to 4.9°C with a mean around 2°C for doubling the CO_2 concentration to 600 ppm. As there is a

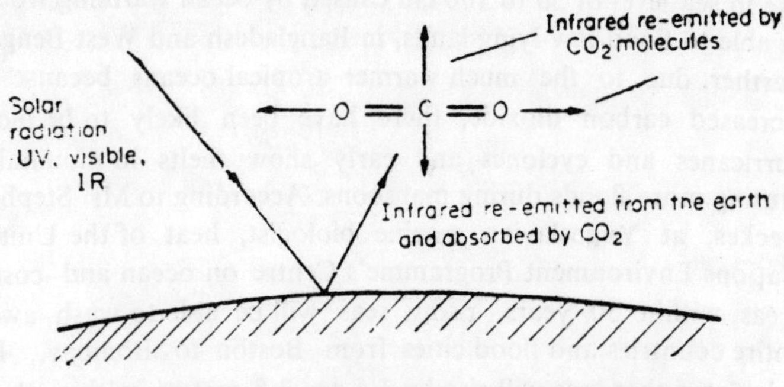

Fig. 3.4. A schematic drawing illustrating the greenhouse effect Infrared radiation from the earth absorbed by CO_2 molecules is re-emitted in all directions returning some back to the earth's surface.

logarithmic relationship between surface temperature and CO_2 concentration it is likely that a temperature will be reached, beyond which further increases of CO_2 levels have little effect. A maximum increase of 2.5K has been suggested. Since 1945 the mean global temperature has dropped suggesting that either the greenhouse effect is not a satisfactory explanation, or some other effect is beginning to dominate. Aerosols in the size range 0.1-5 μm, could reduce incoming radiation by 10% through back scattering and any increase could lead to cooling of the atmosphere. The rate of increase of atmospheric turbidity has been greater than the increase in CO_2 levels, and it could be that this is the more important factor today. It is not yet possible to adequately explain the change in the temperature over the last century, but at least an increase in the CO_2 and aerosol content of the atmosphere has the potential to alter the world's climate. Pollutants such as N_2O, CH_4 and CCl_3F, which have strong infrared absorptions, could also influence the mean global temperature.

An increased heating of earth would cause recede of glaciers, disappearance of ice caps such as those found over Antarctic and Greenland, and rise in ocean level. Infact, it has been estimated that if all the ice on the earth should melt, 200 feet of water would be added to the surface of all oceans, and lowlying costal cities such as Bangkok and Venice would get inundated. Only a rise in sea level of 50 to 100 cm caused by ocean warming would be able to flood low-lying lands, in Bangladesh and West Bengal. Further, due to the much warmer tropical oceans because of increased carbon dioxide, there have been likely to be more hurricanes and cyclones and early show melts in mountains causing more floods during mansoons. According to Mr. Stephan Keckes, at Yugoslavian marine biologist, heat of the United Nations Environment Programme's Centre on ocean and costal areas, within 30 years, rising seas will be able to wash away entire countries and flood cities from Boston to Bombay. He calculated that seas will rise by 1.5 to 3.5 meters within three decades. In Bangladesh alone 15 million people will have to move or drown. He says that little can be done about rising, oceans beyond studying the phenomenon and preparing for the worst.

According to G.N. Plass, if the carbon dioxide content of the atmosphere gets doubled, the average surface temperature of the earth would rise 6.5°F (see Franke and Franke, 1975). However, this would not happen because of reflection of some of the sun's heat back into the space by densely accumulating particulate contaminants such as smoke and dust from industrial and automobile exhaust. If carbon dioxide continues to accumulate, it may disallow the cooling effect of particulate contaminants, and as a consequence the earth's temperature may rise again.

There is sufficient evidence that the temperature of the entire earth has risen slighty during recent decades. Glaciers in both hemisphere are receding. Between 1885 to 1940, there occurred an increase in mean annual temperature of about 0.9°F of the earth. After 1940, global warming subsided. Warming of Northern Europe and North America continued between 1940 and 1960, but the mean annual air temperature on global scale as well as for the Northern Hemisphere got decreased slightly (0.2°F). More than 40 per cent of the total increase in carbon dioxide content of the atmosphere from combustion occurred during that period. It might be possible that increased particulate pollutants from industry and automobile exhaust nullified or masked any effect of temperature from carbon dioxide content of the atmosphere, but this has been not. There was an overall temperature rise of 0.7°C over the past 134 years with the three warmest years in the whole record being 1980, 1981 and 1982. In addition, five of the nine warmest years even have occurred since 1978. There have been however, some unexplained fluctuations within this long term trend, between 1980 and the mid-1980 but overall conditions were relatively steady, with land-based readings actually showing a slight fall. The latest predictions for global warming given at European meetings of climatologists and policy makers say that the temperature of the earth could increase by 1.5 to 4.5°C by the year 2050 (The Time of India, December 9, 1986).

The trend in temperature which has taken place over the last century cannot be associated with the postulated increase in CO_2 concentration over the same period. Average northern hemisphere temperatures increased by 0.6°C between 1890 and 1940 but since that date have decreased by 0°C. This does not rule out the relationship between CO_2 concentrations and temperature but reveals the uncertainty associated with prediction of climatic change and the magnitude of natural effects of unknown cause.

It has been assumed that particulate concentrations have been increasing because of man's activities and that this increase would have an effect of the climate Particles, for instance, increase, the albedo (percentage of sunlight reflected) by scattering the incoming radiation, and cooling would be predicted as a consequence. Particles also scatter the outgoing radiation, although not so effectively because the particulate sizes that predominate in the atmosphere are most efficient at scattering light of the incoming wavelengths.

Particles also absorb and re-emit radiation; the wavelengths at which this take place have been a function of the particle composition. In parallel with the greenhouse argument, if this absorption predominated in the infrared region corresponding to the earth's emission, the result would be warming and cooling would ensure on absorption of the sun's emission. Particles, unlike CO_2 are having a relatively short lifetime in the atmosphere, of the order of 3 to 5 days. In addition, the man-made contribution to the atmosphere's total particulate burden have been relatively small (approximately 10%). It is argued that under these circumstances it is unlikely that there may occur any change in particulate concentrations because of man's activities, and that there could not be any associated climatic effect. This is not to say that fluctuations in particulate loading as, for example, take place in the stratosphere following volcanic activity, do not have an influence on climate.

No melting of the ice caps has been observed yet, but some predictions are that these effects could show up in the next 3\-80 years. Some melting might take place, but total conversion of the earth's ice into liquid water seems highly unlikely when the actual energy requirements are considered. For example, the energy given up when 300 litres of air is cooled 1°C (1.8°F) would melt only one gram of ice if the ice was already at the melting temperature.

Some scientists feel that rather than a flood, an ice age is more likely. Their calculations indicate that the cooling of the earth's atmosphere caused by increased particulate pollution makes an ice age a possibility for the future.

Obviously, a number of variables are involved in all of these predictions, and the net effect of atmospheric pollutants on the climate and weather remain to be seen. They could prove to be very profound, or they might even cancel one another out.

4

Hydrosphere

4.1 Introduction

Water is a very complicated and vitally important substance. It is the medium which gave birth to the first primitive living molecules, and without it no life can exist.

Throughout history, the quality and quantity of water available to man have been vital factors in ascertaining his well-being. Whole civilizations have disappeared due to water shortages resulting from changes in climate, and the process continues today with the starvation of African peoples as the Sahara marches southward. Disastrous floods have always plagued mankind. Waterborne diseases are able to kill millions of people although in the more well-developed areas of the world, the great plagues of cholera and typhoid have been controlled. Ambitious programs of dam and dike construction have reduced flood damage, though not without undesirable side effects. However, problems with water remain, and in some respects have been becoming more serious.

Any consideration of environmental chemistry as applied to water needs some understanding of the sources, transport, characteristics, and composition of water. The chemical reactions taking place in water, and the chemical species found in it, get influenced strongly by the environment in which the water is found. The chemistry of water exposed to the atmosphere has been quite different from that of water at the bottom of a lake. Microorganisms play a vital role in determining the chemical composition of water. Thus in discussing water chemistry, one must discuss the many general factors which are able to influence this chemistry.

4.2 Hydrological Cycle

The hydrologic cycle refers to the process in which water gets converted from its solid or liquid state into vapor state. In the vapor state water is capable of travelling considerable distances from its source prior to recondensing and returning to earth as precipitation. Hence the hydrologic cycle has been a complex, interelated system which involves the movement of atmospheric, surface (marine and fresh), and groundwater throughout various regions of the world. It has been the hydrologic cycle which has been solely responsible for the world's precipitation, and due to this precipitation, falling on the terrestrial and surface freshwater, environments, that has been the sole source of the earth's supply of fresh water (Fig. 4.1).

The hydrologic cycle may be having either a long or various short cycles. In the short cycles, water may evaporate from either marine or freshwater systems, condense almost immediately, and return as precipitation to the same system. Another variation of a short cycle has been the precipitation and subsequent evaporation of water from land surfaces, which has been followed by its condensation and return as precipitation to the land, followed by reevaporation, and so on.

All the water which is present within surface zone of the Earth, 97% of it is in the oceans about 20% is in ice caps and glaciers, which cover only 10% of the present land surface, and only 0.6% is fresh water available for direct use to humans. The water cycle is governed by the absorption of solar energy, most of which causes evaporation of water from the oceans and land though a small proportion generates the winds, waves

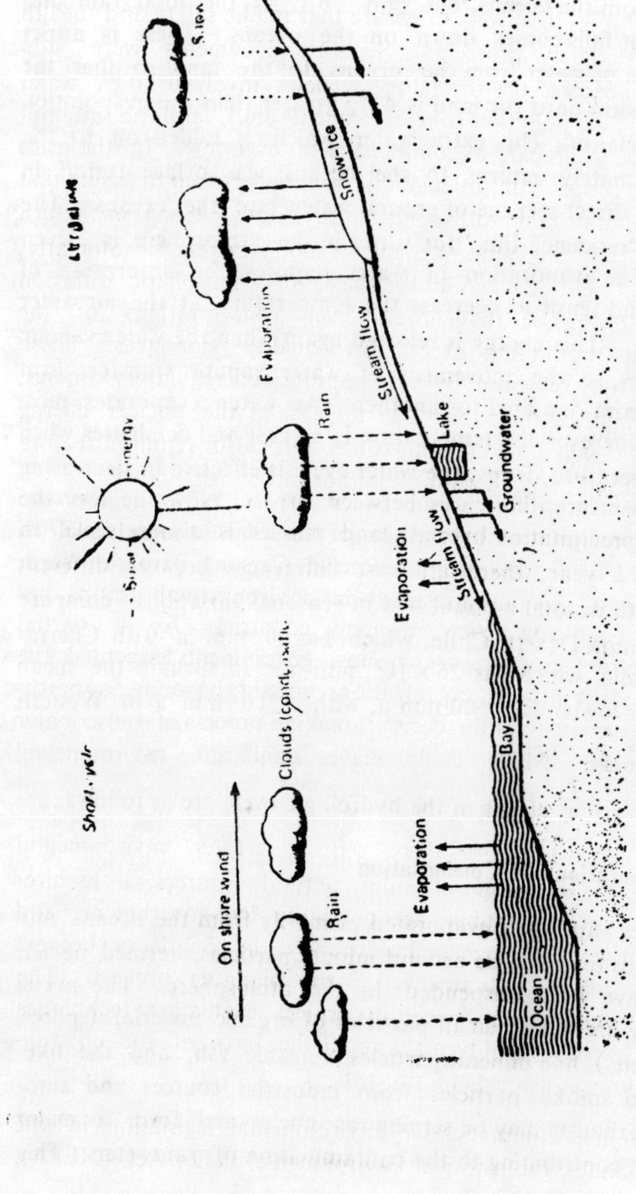

Fig. 4.1. The Hydrologic Cycle

and currents which help the circulation in both the atmosphere and water masses. 83% of the water which is evaporated comes from the oceans, but only 76% of the total rain and snow that falls comes down on the oceans. There is a net migration of water from the oceans to the land so that the precipitation onto the land is 43% greater than the evaporation from the land. The extra water which is added on to the land ultimately returns to the oceans via surface runoff in rivers or direct seepage of ground water into the oceans. The average 'residence time' for water in the atmosphere is eleven days. The evaporation of water requires the absorption of energy and tends to decrease the temperature at the air/water interface. This energy is released again when the water vapour condenses, so the movement of water vapour transfers heat energy from one area to another. As water evaporates most readily wherever the temperature is highest and condenses when the temperature drops, the water cycle is effective in decreasing the temperature differences between areas. Now the less the average precipitation over all land masses is almost equal to 700 mm a year, there are vast differences between different areas both in total amount and in seasonal variations—compare the Atacama Desert, Chile, which has 0 mm a with Cherrapunji, India, which has 26×10^3 mm a. In Britain the mean value for lowlands is 500 mm a, with 2500 mm a in Western hill areas.

The various stages in the hydrologic cycle are as follows :

(i) Evaporation and Condensation

Water vapor gets evaporated primarily from the oceans and then tends to condense around minute particles, termed nuclei, which have been suspended in the atmosphere. The nuclei generally are having small particles of organic material (spores, pollen, etc.), fine mineral particles, volcanic ash, and the like. Dust and smoke particles from industrial sources and automotive exhausts may be serving as nuclei and form a major factor in contributing to the contamination of rainwater. This is due to the fact that airborne particles (such as lead) readily dissolve in the newly condensed atmospheric water, and these materials then gets returned to earth along with the rain water.

Initially, the condensed liquid has been in the form of extremely small droplets [less than 0.04 millimetre (mm) in diameter]. Due to their small size, their rate of fall has been negligible, and they get retained in the atmosphere as clouds. Finally, however, this vapor forms precipitation in response to one of three major factors. The largest amount of precipitation would be formed when masses of warm, moist air move into regions of cold air. This causes a rapid condensation of the vapor and subsequent precipitation. The second factor arises during periods of warm weather, when air, warmed at the earth's surface, gets decreased in density and rises into overlying cold air, bringing about condensation of the water vapor. The third mechanism involved in condensation takes place with the cooling of air masses as they move over high mountains. In each case the cooling of warm, moist air has been responsible for the condensation and precipitation of rainwater.

(ii) Runoff, Stream Flow, and Infiltration

When rain is falling on a terrestrial area, a portion of the water would be caught by vegetation. This process is known as interception and this water readily get reevaporated, as there is a larger surface area that is exposed to wind action. The remainder of the water falls to earth, and a portion sinks into the soil surface by a process known as infiltration. The portion not infiltrated into the soil, called surface runoff, flows over the surface and gets discharged (in undeveloped areas) into streams. The water entering a stream by surface runoff plus the water entering via groundwater flow is known as runoff. Thus the terms "runoff" and "surface runoff" have been different and distinct. Surface runoff equals precipitation minus the water lost by interception and infiltration. Runoff, on the other hand, has been generally synonymous with stream flow and has been equal to the sum of the surface water plus the groundwater that enters a stream.

Infiltration has been somewhat also distinct from groundwater when the water percolates into the earth's surface, different portions would be following three distinct pathways. A portion of the water will function as interflow, since the presence of impermeable lower sediments will disallow deep penetration of this water. Consequently, this segment will flow just below the soil surface and discharge into streams. Another portion would be remaining above the water table in an area called the zone of unsaturated flow. Both of these portions of water are regarded to be in the zone of aeration. The third portion will percolate down into the groundwater table and will, eventually, get discharged into streams.

(iii) Evapotranspiration

A large amount of the precipitated water would be converted to vapor by evaporation and/or transpiration. Evaporation refers to the process whereby molecules of liquid water (at the surface of a water body or in moist soil) absorb sufficient energy to leave the liquid state and enter the vapor state. The energy absorbed by the water in this process gets stored within the vapor—hence somewhat large amount of heat contained in the moist air.

Transpiration refers to the process whereby terrestrial and emergent aquatic vegetation release water vapor to the atmosphere. In the process of photosynthesis all plants have been taking in liquid water and carbon dioxide and, by a complex series of reactions, convert these materials to carbohydrate, oxygen (gas), and water vapor. Sub-mergent aquatic vegetation (plants growing completely beneath the water surface) also liberates water and oxygen as vapors but, in these cases, the oxygen and water vapor produced and released into the surrounding liquid water would immediately form hydrogen bonds with the liquid water. The water vapor will get converted to its liquid form, whereas the oxygen remains in the water column as dissolved oxygen. As the leaves of both terrestrial and aquatic emergent vegetation have been in air, the water vapor and oxygen, when released by these plants in photosynthesis, will remain in the vapor state as there are insufficient water molecules in the immediate vicinity to form hydrogen bonds and keep the water vapor and oxygen in solution.

The water converted from liquid to vapor in transpiration has been quite considerable, and the ability of plants to remove water from both soil and aquatic systems cannot be under-estimated. Transpiration by emergent vegetation has been a major factor in the "drying up" of lakes.

Groundwater, unless it has been within a few feet of the surface, could not be evaporated. Rather, the portion that gete converted to vapour gets transpired by plants. In most regions the water lost by evaporation cannot be measured separately from the water lost transpiration. Consequently, the two are regarded together as evapotranspiration.

(iv) Ground Water

The most lengthy portion of the hydrologic cycle would get completed when groundwater gets returned to the earth's surface. The return may take place by springs, transpiration, or by artificial means.

Any natural surface discharge of sufficient water that will flow as a small rivulet is known as a spring, while a smaller discharge is known as surface seepage. Groundwater may also be discharged as subaqueous springs below the surface of lakes, rivers, and marine systems. It is possible to classify springs generally on the basis of their magnitude of discharge, as summarized in Table 5.1. Three major factors affecting the magnitude of a spring have been the land area accepting the rainfall and thus contributing water to the sub-surface system, the permeability of the soil and subsoil, and the quantity of water entering the system (the amount of recharge). The use of water, in developed areas, prior to recharge has been known to alter the quality and quantity of the water entering the sub-surface system.

Table 4.1

Classification of Spring Discharge

Magnitude	*Discharge*
First	Greater than 2.83 m^3/s
Second	0.283-2 83 m^3/s
Third	2.83-283 litres/s
Fourth	2.83-6.31 litres/s
Fifth	6.31-0.631 litres/s
Sixth	6.31-6.31 l. l/s
Seventh	7.9-63.1 ml/s
Eighth	Less than 7.9 ml/s

Discussions

All three phases of water (solid, liquid and gas) are available on the Earth's surface. The formula of water, H_2O, indicates a molecular weight of 18. If we see at other covalently bonded molecules with similar molecular weights (*e.g.* CO and NO) we find that they have boiling points below the normal temperature range, say 258 K to 323 K (– 15°C to 50°C), found on the Earth.

The water used by man is primarily fresh surface water and ground water. In arid regions a small fraction of man's water supply comes from the ocean, a source which is likely to become more important as the world's supply of fresh water dwindles relative to demand. Saline or brackish ground waters may also be used in some areas.

Ground water and surface water are having appreciably different characteristics. Many substances either dissolve in surface water or get suspended in it on its path to the ocean.

Surface water collected in a lake or reservior, and having the mineral nutrients essential for algae growth may support a heavy growth of alge. Surface water having a high level of biodegradable organic material normally contains a high population of bacteria. All these factors are having a profound effect upon the quality of surface water.

Ground water is able to dissolve minerals from the formations through which it passes. Most microorganisms originally present in ground water are slowly filtered out as it seeps through the ground. Occasionally, the content of undesirable salts may become excessively high in ground water, although generally it has been superior to surface water for use by man as a domestic water source.

4.3 Unique Properties of Water

The study of water is termed as hydrology. This is divided into a number of subcategories :

(i) Limnology. It is the branch of the science which deals with the characteristics of fresh water, including biological properties as well as chemical and physical properties.

(ii) Oceanography. It is the science of ocean and its properties.

Water is having a number of unique properties, without which life could not exist. Many of these properties have been due to hydrogen bonding in water. It has been an excellent solvent for many materials. Thus water is the basic transport medium for the nutrients and waste products involved in life processes. The extremely high dielectric constant of water compared to other liquids is having a profound effect upon the solvent properties of water, in that most ionic materials are dissociated in water. With the exception of liquid ammonia, water is having the highest heat capacity of any liquid or solid, 1 cal $\times$ g^{-1} $\times$ $deg.^{-1}$. Due to this high heat capacity, a relatively large amount of heat is needed to ch nge the temperature of a mass of water appreciably, which can have a stabilizing effect upon the temperature of whole geographic regions. In addition, it does not allow sudden large changes of temperature in large bodies of water, and thereby protects aquatic organisms from the shock of abrupt temperature variations. The extremely high heat of vaporization of water, 585 cal/g at 20°C, likewise helps to stabilize the temperature of bodies of water and the surrounding geographic regions. It also influences the transfer of heat and water vapor between bodies of water and the atmosphere. Water is having its maximum density at a temperature (4°C) above its freezing point. The fortunate consequence of that fact has been that ice floats so that few large bodies of water ever freeze solid. Furthermore, the pattern of vertical circulation of water in lakes, a determining factor in their chemistry and biology, governed largely by the unique temperature-density relationship of water.

4.4 Biological Method of Zonation

As sunlight has been such an important factor in the productivity of these systems, it has been customary to divide both marine and freshwater systems into definite zones on the basis of the depth of sunlight penetration. This has been primarily a biological method of zonation. The various wavelengths of light are rapidly filtered out as they pass through a water column. Based upon the degree of light penetration, it has been possible to divide a system into certain zones (Fig. 4.2).

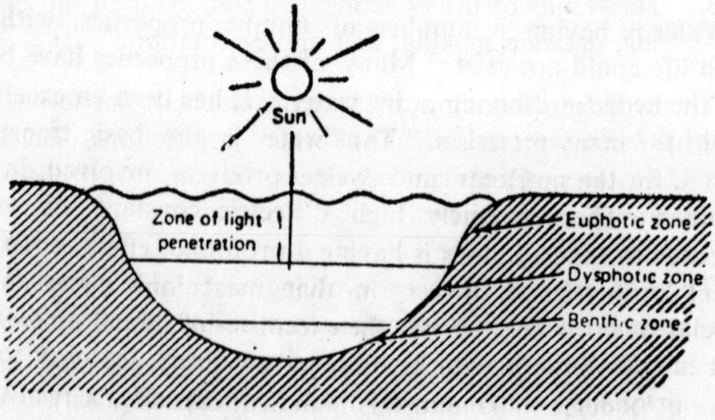

Fig. 4.2. Lake zonation on the basis of sunlight penetration

The upper zone of sunlight penetration is known as the euphotic zone. Beneath this is a zone of perpetual darkness, the dysphotic zone, which is extending from the bottom of the euphotic zone to the bottom. The bottom sediment underlying the dysphotic zone is known as the benthic zone and the regeneration zone.

According to this type of classification, shallow lakes, streams, and rivers would not behaving a dysphotic zone, as they would be shallow enough to allow for sunlight penetration down to the benthic zone. In addition, the position of both the euphtioc and dysphotic zone in deep systems generally shifts with environmental conditions. For example, during periods of heavy rainfall, when sediment has been washed into the system, the physical presence of this suspended sediment would tend to block the sunlight, bringing about a reduction of the euphotic zone and an increase of the dysphotic zone.

In typical aquatic and marine systems the euphotic zone has been regarded to be both the zone of sunlight penetration and the zone of oxygen and food production. It has been in this zone that the plants and the primary consumers would be found, at least during the periods of active photosynthesis and grazing. The other consumers (secondary, tertiary, etc.) would occur in all three zones, depending upon the availability of their food source.

4.5 Lotic Environment

The lotic environment is consisting of all inland waters in which the entire water body continually moves in a definite direction.' Thus rivers, streams, and brooks are regarded to be lotic environments. These systems have been generally originating from precipitation that falls on the earth's sloping surface and flows downhill as sheet wash. Sheet wash tends to accumulate in low areas and to form intermittent rivulets, which eventually flow into streams. When the water flow continues, it will tend to erode the bed of the stream, making it to intercept the groundwater table and become a permanent stream. As additional streams are formed and eventually meet, the resulting length, depth, and size of the system will warrant classification as a river.

The rivulet-stream sequence can still get observed upstream, but in an ever-changing position, because erosion will make an upstream migration of these features. The migration will continue until halted by a natural feature like a drainage divine. A direct result of this erosion-induced geological migration has been a continual migration of biological habitats. In other words, erosion will make the headwaters to "migrate" upstream which is followed by a similar "migration" of the environmental conditions characteristic of rivulets, streams, and rivers. The animal and plant communities that occupy each of these habitats must also move upstream, to remain in the same habitats (which has been in a constantly changing position because of erosion), or must adapt to the gradually changing conditions brought about by the erosion caused by the running waters. In natural, undisturbed systems these changes have been very slow and permit ample time for the organism to adapt to the changing conditions.

As lotic systems tend to be shallower and narrower than lakes, there has been generally a greater proportion of water exposed to land surfaces. Consequently, streams have been more intimately associated with and affected by the terrestrial environment than have been most lentic systems. In addition, lotic systems have been more dependent on the surrounding land areas for a large proportion of their nutrient supply.

4.6 Lentic Environment

The lentic environment has been including all inland waters in which the water has been not continually flowing in a definite direction. The water in these systems have been essentially standing, although some water motion may take place because of wind-driven waves and/or in the vicinity of inlets and outlets. From a long-term geologic viewpoint, however, these inlets and outlets have been regarded to be temporary impoundments that will in time disappear, converting the system to a flowing-water environment. Typical lentic environments have been regarded to be lakes, ponds, and marshes.

In lentic systems the aging process has been just the reverse of that described for lotic systems. Whereas streams tend to get wider and deeper as they age, lakes tend to get shallower and the banks extend into what was originally open water. Natural filling has been generally due to wind-blown materials (sand, leaves, etc.) entering the system, sediment input by streams, and terrestrial runoff and aquatic plant and animal debris. Not all lentic environments have been becoming shallower by this type of filling alone, however. In many cases outlets may widen and deepen, making an increased outflow of water having a subsequent lowering of the water level.

Lakes could be generally classified, on the basis of their depth and nutrient levels, as oligotrophic, eutrophic, or senescent.

An oligotrophic lake has been regarded to be in its young stage. These lakes have been very deep, with a sand or rock bottom, and have been low in nutrients. Because of the paucity of nutrients, both plant and animal life are low.

Eutrophic lakes have been regarded as middle-aged systems. They have been relatively shallow in comparison to oligotrophic systems, with a silty or mud bottom, and have sufficient nutrients for supporting a large population of plants and animals.

A senescent lake has been in the oldest stage of development. The bottom sediments in senescent systems have been consisting of a thick layer of organic silts and/or muds, nutrient levels are high, and the system has been very shallow. There has been a large percentage of rooted emergent vegetation which is growing throughout the system. Terrestrial or marsh vegetation tends to grow along the banks and into the lake itself over the root mat.

On the basis of temperature (and thus, indirectly, density) lakes could be divided into three distinct zones : the epilimnion, the thermocline, and the hypolimnion (Fig. 5.3). The epilimnion has been the upper zone of gradual temperature change. Below the epilimnion has been a zone of rapid temperature change termed the thermocline. In order for this region to meet the established criterion for classification as a thermocline, the temperature must alter by at least 1°C for every metre of depth. If the temperature changes at a lesser rate relative to depth, these waters would be classified as a portion of the epilimnion. Below the thermocline there has been an area of water that has been constantly at a temperature of 4°C, termed the hypolimnion. As the waters of the hypolimnion have been at 4°C they have been at their maximum density and will occur at the bottom layer in any system. Comparing the relative water temperatures and density variations seasonally, it has been noted that in summer the warmer water will be located in the upper epilimnion and the colder, denser, water will be located in the hypolimnion. In the winter the colder, less dense water at temperatures below 4°C will be located in the hypolimnion. In either case, the less dense water has been in the epilimnion and the dense (4°C) water has been always found in the bottom waters of the hypolimnion.

As water has higher density than ice or when ice meets the density of water increases and its maximum at 4°C. Due to of these density changes the behaviour of water is particularly suits to the preservation of aquatic life-forms. A lake in summer, if sufficiently deep, becomes stratified (Fig. 4.3). Because of the poor conductivity of the water which allows the warming up of the surface layers which become less dense compared to the cooler lower layers. As the two layers do not mix, the lower layer (hypolimnion) will tend to become oxygen-deficient at the organic matter present gets oxidised. At the same time the upper layer (epilimnion) can become deficient in nutrients, because the living organisms remove the nutrients from the water and then, on dying, fall to the lake bottom, taking the consumed nutrients with them. In the autumn, air temperatures drop and the surface layers of the lake cool down. When the upper layers (epilimnion) temperature drops to that of the lower layer (hypolimnion) the stratification disappears and vertical mixing, or turnover, occurs (Fig. 4.3b). This allows oxygenation of all the water and carries nutrients up from the lower levels to the surface. As the air temperature goeson decreasing, the surface water temperature goes

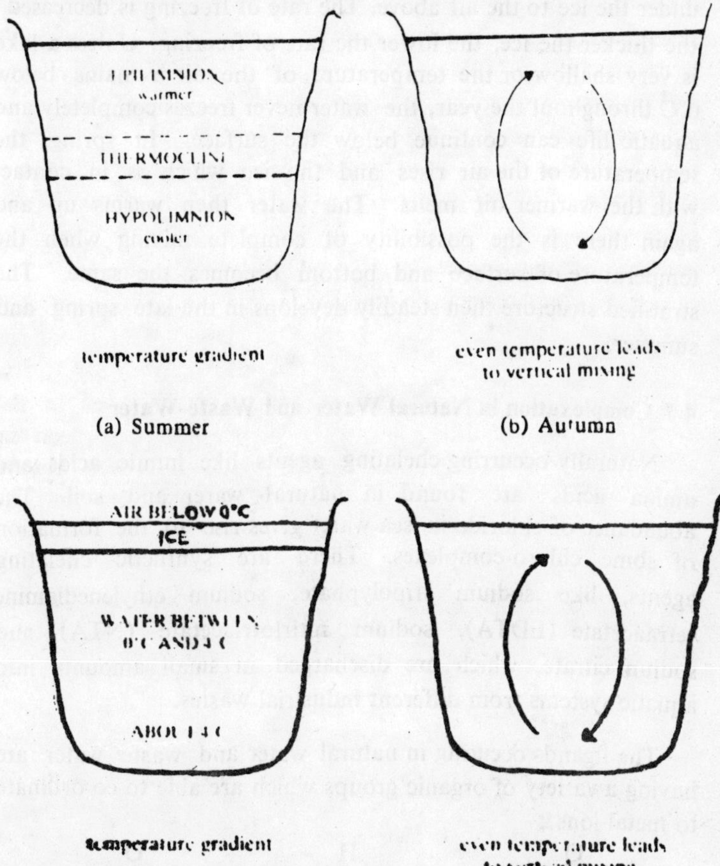

Fig. 4.3. The thermal stratification and mixing of lakes at diffrent times of the year.

below 4°C and the surface layer is again less dense than the bottom layer at 4°C. When the surface temperature becomes 0°C, ice will be formed on the surface, which leads to the release of energy as the extra hydrogen bonds are formed : this energy is responsible for the rise in temperature of the water below the ice. Once the ice covers the surface, it behaves as an insulating layer thereby reducing the heat loss from the water under the ice to the air above. The rate of freezing is decreased : the thicker the ice, the lower the rate of freezing. Unless a lake is very shallow or the temperature of the air remains below 0°C throughout the year, the water never freezes completely and aquatic life can continue below the surface. In spring, the temperature of the air rises and the ice which is in contact with the warmer air melts. The water then warms up and again there is the possibility of complete mixing when the temperature of surface and bottom becomes the same. The stratified structure then steadily develops in the late spring and summer.

4.7 Complexation in Natural Water and Waste Water

Naturally occurring chelating agents like humic acids and amina acids are found in natural warer and soil. The abundance of chloride in sea water gives rise to the formation of some chloro-complexes. There are synthetic chelating agents, like sodium tripolyphate, sodium ethylenediamine tetraacetate (EDTA), sodium nitirlotriacetate (NTA) and sodium citrate, which are discharged in small amounts into aquatic systems from different industrial wastes.

The ligands occuring in natural water and waste water are having a variety of organic groups which are able to co-ordinate to metal ions :

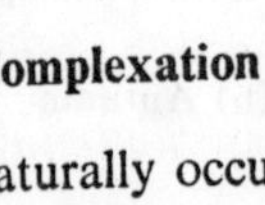

Carboxylate group

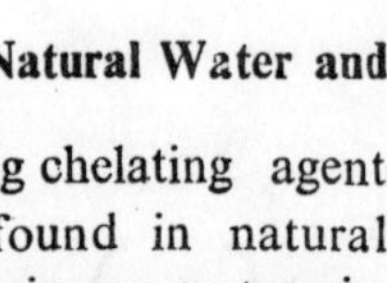

aliphatic and aromatic amino group

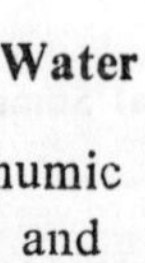

phenoxide group

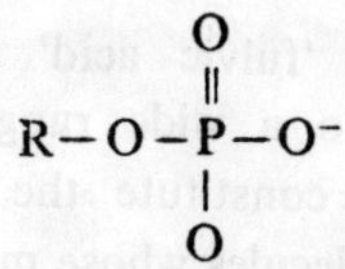

Phosphate group

These ligands are known to form complexes with most metal ions (Mg^{2+}, Ca^{2+}, Mn^{2+}, Fe^{3+}, Cu^{2+}, Zn^{2+}, CO^{2+}, Ni^{2+} Sr^{2+}, Cd^{2}, and Ba^{2+}) which are present in natural water and biological systems.

4.8 Humic Substances

These are the complexing agents which are important and found in nature. Although their existence has been known since 1800, yet their structural and chemical properties have been still challenging chemists.

Humic substances have been non-degradable materials which are formed during the decomposition of vegetation. They are found as deposits in soil, marsh sediments and any location where there have occurred large quantities of vegetation.

They are generally classified on the basis of solubility. If a humic substance could be extracted with a strong base and the resulting solution acidified the products have been (a) a non-extractable plant residue termed as humin, (b) a material which gets precipitated from the acidified extract, termed as humic acid and (c) an organic material which is left in the acidified solution, called fulvic acid. The properties of water have been mainly affected by the humic substances, both soluble and insoluble because of their acid-base, adsorptive and complexing properties. The soluble fulvic acid is having an effect on the properties of water, while the insoluble humin and humic acids are able to alter water quality by involving exchange of cations, organic materials, etc., with water.

The elementary composition of humic substances C. 45−55%; O, 30−45%; H, 3−6%; N, 1−5% and S, 0−1%.

'Humin', humic acid, and 'fulvic acid' are not applicable to single compounds but to a wide range of compounds. In general, humic substances constitute the high-molecular-weight polyelectrolytic macromolecules whose molecular weights range from a few hundred (fulvic acids) to tens of thousands (humic acid and humin fractions).

They are having a carbon skeleton with a high degree of aromatic character and a large percentage of functional groups having oxygen. They may also be having protein-like materials and a carbohydrate fraction. These fractions can readily get hydrolyzed from the aromatic nucleus which is able to withstand chemical and biochemical attack.

When these occurs the decomposition of humic acid, the following typical decomposition products are obtained :

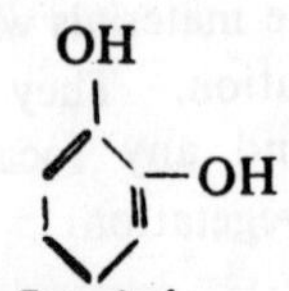

Catechol

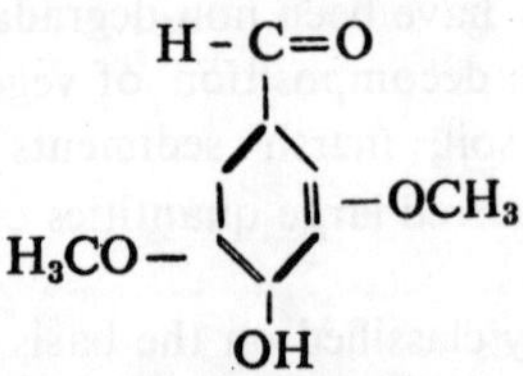

Syringaldehyde

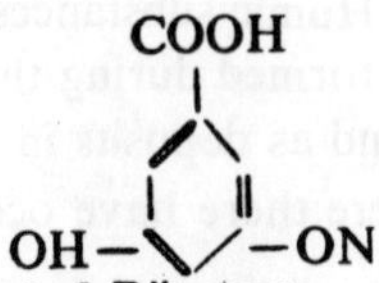

3, 5-Dihydroxy benzoic acid

The hypothetical structural formula of fulvic acid may be put as follows :

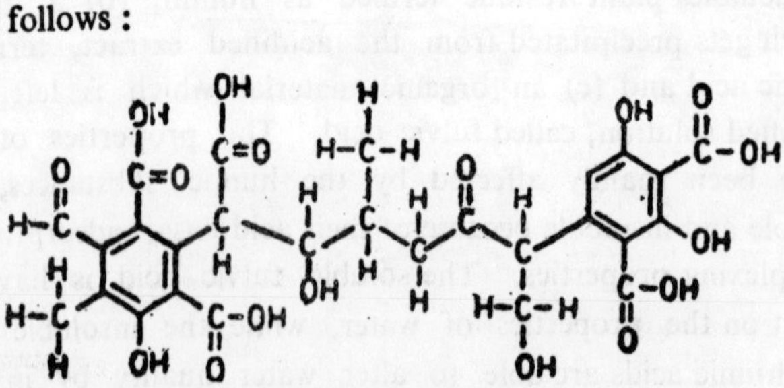

Fulvic acid

The fulvic acid is having a formula weight 666 and chemical formula, $C_{20}\ H_{15}\ (COOH)_6\ (OH)_5\ (CO)_2$.

Humic substances are able to chelate metal ions through a carboxyl and a phenolic hydroxyl group.

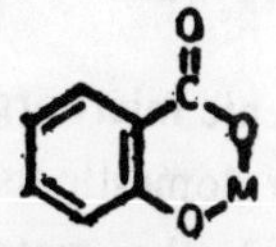

phenolic hydroxyl group

with two carboxyl groups,

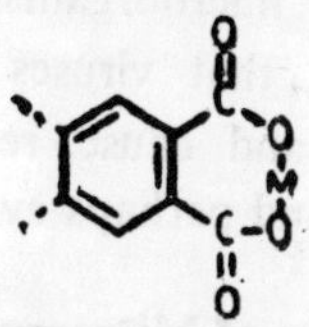

carboxyl group

or with a carboxyl group,

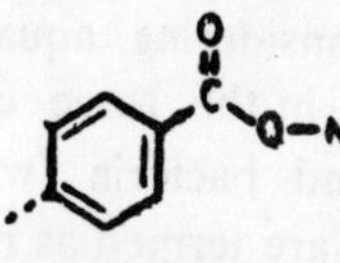

carboxyl group

Insoluble humic substances such as the humic and humic acids are able to exchange cations with water and are having the capacity to accumulate large amounts of metals.

4.9 Micro-Organic—The Catalyst of Aquatic Chemical Reactions

Microorganisms such as the bacteria, fungi, and algae have been living catalysts which are able to being about a vast number of chemical processes in water and soil. A majority of the important chemical reactions taking place in water, particularly those involving organic matter and oxidation-reduction processes, take place through bacterial intermediaries. Algae constitute the primary producers of biological organic matter (biomass) in water. Microorganisms have been considered to be responsible for the formation of many sediment and mineral deposits. Algae photosynthesis increases the pH of water thus causing the formation of calcium carbonate deposits. Some anaerobic bacteria produce hydrogen sulfide which reacts with metal ions to produce sulfide mineral deposits. With present technology, microorganisms are able to play the dominant role in secondary waste treatment.

Pathogenic microorganism must be eliminated from water purified for domestic use because the major epidemics of typhoid, cholera, and other water-borne diseases have been resulted from pathogenic microorganisms in water supplies. There is some speculation that viruses in water escape conventional water treatment and cause respiratory and digestive tract diseases, hepatitis, and perhaps even some forms of cancer.

4.10 Types of Microorganisms in Waters

In considering aquatic chemistry. microorganisms may be included in the three categories of bacteria, fungi, and algae. Fungi and bacteria (with the exception of photosynthetic bacteria) are termed as reducers. Reducers break down chemical compounds to more simple species, and thereby extract the energy needed for their growth and for their metabolic needs. As reducers can utilize only chemical energy, and chemical transformation mediated by them must involve a net loss of free energy. However, compared to higher organisms, the energy utilization of bacteria and fungi has been very efficient.

Algae have been classified as producers, as they use light energy and store it as chemical energy. In the absence of sunlight, however, algae use chemical energy for their metabolic needs. In a sense, therefore, bacteria and fungi may be looked upon as environmental catalysts, while algae are aquatic "solar fuel cells." Some of the chemical relationships among microorganisms have been depicted in Fig. 4.4.

Algae may be regarded as generally microscopic organisms which subsist on inorganic nutrients and produce organic matter from carbon dioxide by photosynthesis. The general nutrient requirements of algae are carbon (from CO_2 or HCO_3^-), nitrogen (generally as NO_3^-), phosphorus (as some form of orthophosphate), sulfur (as SO_4^{2-}), and trace elements such as sodium, potassium, calcium, magnesium, iron, cobalt, and molybdenum.

In a highly simplified form, the production of organic matter by algae photosynthesis may be put by the equation

$$CO_2 + H_2O \xrightarrow{h\nu} (CH_2O) + O_2 \uparrow \qquad \text{.. (4.1)}$$

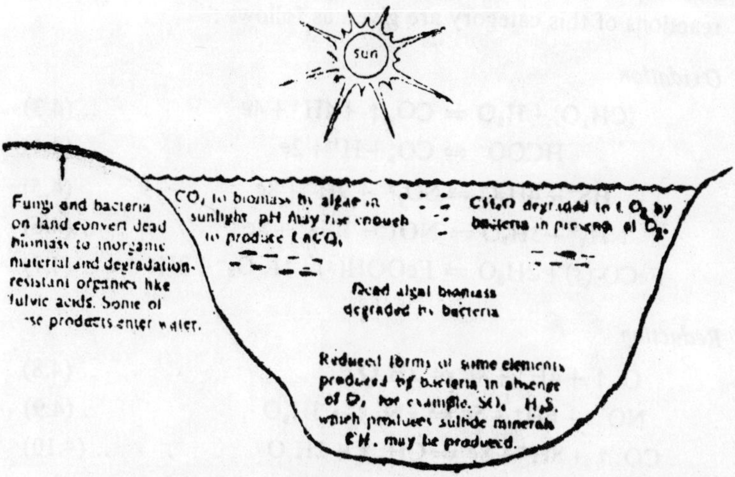

Fig. 4.4. Effects of microorganisms on the chemistry of water

where CH_2O denotes a unit of carbohydrate and $h\nu$ stands for the energy of a quantum of light. Fogg (1) has represented the overall formula of the algae, Chlorella, as $C_{5.7}H_{9.8}O_{2.3}N$ (including phosphorus the formula would be $C_{5.7}H_{9.8}O_{2.3}NP_{0.06}$). Using Fogg's formula for algae biomass, the overall reaction for photosynthesis may be the following :

$$5.7CO_2 + 3.4H_2O + NH_3 \xrightarrow{h\nu} C_{5.7}H_{9.8}O_{2.3}N + 6.25O_2 \quad \text{...(4.2)}$$

In the absence of light, algae are able to metabolize organic matter in the same manner as do nonphotosynthetic organisms. Thus, algae may be able to satisfy their metabolic demands by using chemical energy from the degradation of stored starches or oils, or from the consumption of algae protoplasm itself. In the absence of photosynthesis the metabolic process uses oxygen, so that during the hours of darkness an aquatic system having a heavy growth of algae may get depleted in oxygen.

4.11 Microbially Mediated Redox Reactions

Bacteria are able to mediate a variety of redox reactions and thereby drive the energy are able to for their metabolic processes and reproduction. Some environmentally important redox reactions of this category are given as follows :

Oxidation

$$\{CH_2O\} + H_2O \rightleftharpoons CO_2\uparrow + 4H^+ + 4e \quad \ldots(4.3)$$

$$HCOO^- \rightleftharpoons CO_2 + H^+ + 2e \quad (4.4)$$

$$HS^- + 4H_2O \rightleftharpoons SO_4^{2-} + 9H^+ + 8e \quad (4.5)$$

$$NH_4^+ + 3H_2O \rightleftharpoons NO_3^- + 10H^+ + 8e \quad \ldots(4.6)$$

$$FeCO_3(s) + 2H_2O \rightleftharpoons FeOOH(s) + HCO_3^- + 2H^+ + e \quad \ldots(4.7)$$

Reduction

$$O_2\uparrow + 4H^+ + 4e \rightleftharpoons 2H_2O \quad \ldots(4.8)$$

$$NO_3^- + 6H^+ + 5e \rightleftharpoons \tfrac{1}{2}N_2\uparrow + 3H_2O \quad \ldots(4.9)$$

$$CO_2\uparrow + 8H^+ + 8e \rightleftharpoons CH_4\uparrow + 2H_2O \quad \ldots(4.10)$$

Bacteria have been taking fact in many biogeochemical processes in water and soil and in many important elemental cycles in nature, such as those of nitrogen, carbon and sulphur. They help in the formation of many mineral deposits including some of those of iron and manganese. Bacteria have been also instrumental in the formation of iron and manganese deposits in natural water systems and pipes used for transporting water.

4.12 Nitrogen Fixation

The biochemical pathway of nitrogen fixation by which atmospheric N_2 is chemically bound in biological or simple inorganic compounds is not simple, and a number of conflicting theories have been advanced to explain the mechanisms of the process. Tracer studies of this vital process by which atmospheric nitrogen gets incorporated into living matter revealed that the first detectable fixed nitrogen species has been NH_3. The ammonia has been then converted rapidly to glutamic and aspartic acids by involving the following reactions :

$$\underset{\alpha\text{-Ketoglutaric acid}}{HO_2C-\overset{\overset{\displaystyle O}{\|}}{C}-CH_2-CH_2-CO_2H} + NH_4^+ + H^+ + 2e =$$

$$\underset{\text{glutanic acid}}{{}^{(-)}O_2C-\overset{\overset{\displaystyle NH_3^{(+)}}{|}}{CH}-CH_2-CH_2-CO_2H} + H_2O \quad .. (4.1)$$

$$\underset{\text{Fumaric acid}}{HO_2C-CH=CH-CO_2H} + NH_4 = \underset{\text{aspartic acid}}{{}^{(-)}O_2C-\overset{\overset{\displaystyle NH_3^{(+)}}{|}}{C}-CH_2CO_2H} \quad .. (4.2)$$

Few kinds of aquatic microorganisms are having the ability to fix atmospheric nitrogen. Among the aquatic bacteria which are having this capability have been photosynthetic bacteria Azotobacter, and several varieties of Clostridium. Among the algae, blue-green algae are able to fix atmospheric nitrogen. In most natural fresh water systems, however, the fraction of nitrogen fixed by organisms in the water relative to that originating from the decay of organic material, fertilizer runoff, and other external sources, has been quite low.

The best known and most important form of nitrogen-fixing bacteria has been Rhizobium, which has a symbiotic (mutually advantageous) relationship with leguminous plants such as clover or alfalfa. The Rhizobium bacteria occur in root nodules, special structures attached to the roots of legumes. These bacteria are able to fix atmospheric nitrogen in a chemical form which the legumes can utilize. When the die and decay, some of the nitrogen gets converted by microorganisms in the decay process to nitrate ion, which may be utilized by other plants. Before the advent of commercial chemical fertilizers, the growth of leguminous crops was widely used as a means of building soil fertility. Some of the nitrate produced by the decay of legumes enters natural waters. In an indirect way, therefore, Rhizobium bacteria have been responsible for the introduction of some nitrogen into waters.

4.13 Nitrification

Nitrification, the conversion of N(– III) to N(V), has been a very common and extremely important process in water and in soil. As it is known aquatic nitrogen in thermodynamic equilibrium with air has been in the form of NO_3 ion, N(V), whereas in most biological compounds nitrogen occur as N(– III), such as $-NH_2$ in amino acids. The equilibrium constant for the overall nitrification reaction, written as one electron-mole,

$$\frac{1}{4}O_2 + \frac{1}{8}NH_4^+ \rightarrow \frac{1}{8}NO_3^- + \frac{1}{4}H^+ + \frac{1}{8}H_2O \qquad (4.1)$$

is $10^{7.59}$ so the reaction is highly favored from a thermodynamic viewpoint.

One of the most important ramifications of this conversion has been that nitrogen gets absorbed by plants primarily as nitrate. When fertilizers are applied in the form of ammonium salts or anhydrous ammonia, a microbial transformation to nitrate enables maximum assimilation of nitrogen by the plants.

If extensive aeration has been allowed to take place in the activated sludge sewage treatment process the ammonia nitrogen in the sewage is largely oxidized to nitrate ion. As the sewage sludge settles out in the settler, the bacteria in the sludge use this nitrate as an oxygen source producing N_2 gas. The bubbles of nitrogen gas bring about the sludge to rise, so that it does not settle properly. This can hinder the proper treatment of sewage through carryover of sludge into effluent water.

In nature, nitrification gets catalyzed by two groups of bacteria, Nitrosomonas and Nitrobacter. Nitrosomonas bacteria cause the transition of ammonia to nitrite,

$$NH_3 + \frac{3}{2}O_2 \rightarrow H^+ + NO_2^- + H_2 \qquad ...(4.2)$$

whereas Nitrobacter mediate the oxidation of nitrite to nitrate :

$$NO_2^- + \frac{1}{2}O_2 \rightarrow NO_3^- \qquad ...(4.3)$$

Both of these highly specialized types of bacteria are obligate aerobes, that is, they function only in the presence of molecular O_2. These bacteria are also chemolithotrophic, implying that they can use oxidizable inorganic materials as electron donors in oxidation reactions to yield needed energy for metabolic processes. A majority of chemolithotrophic bacteria use CO_2 as a carbon source in the synthesis of their biomass and have been therefore, autotrophic. There have been several classes of chemolithotrophic bacteria besides the nitrifying bacteria. These other classes include hydrogen bacteria, colorless sulfur bacteria, and iron bacteria.

For the aerobic conversion of ammoniacal nitrogen to nitrite ion at pH 7.00,

$$\frac{1}{6}NH_4^+ + \frac{1}{4}O_2(g) \rightarrow \frac{1}{6}NO_2^- + \frac{1}{3}H^+ + \frac{1}{6}H_2O \quad ...(4.4)$$

the free energy change is 10.8 kcal. The free energy change for the aerobic oxidation of one electron mole of nitrite ion to nitrate ion

$$\frac{1}{2}NO_2^- + \frac{1}{4}O_2(g) \rightarrow \frac{1}{2}NO_3^- \quad (4.5)$$

has been -9.0 kcal. Both steps of the nitrification process involve an appreciable yield of free energy. It has been interesting to note that the free energy yield per electron mole has been approximately the same for the conversion of NH_4^+ to NO_2^- as it is for the conversion of NO_2^- to NO_3^-, about 10 kcal/electron-mole.

4.14 Nitrate Reduction

The general term "nitrate reduction" means the microbial processes by which nitrogen in chemical compounds gets reduced to lower oxidation states. In the absence of free oxygen, nitrate may be used by some bacteria as an alternate electron receptor. The most complete possible reduction of nitrogen in nitrate ion involves the acceptance of 8 electrons by the nitrogen atom with the consequent conversion of nitrate to ammonia (+V to −III oxidation state). Nitrogen is an essential component of protein, and any organism which utilizes nitrogen from nitrate for the synthesis of protein must first reduce the nitrogen to the −III oxidation state (ammoniacal form). However, incorporation of nitrogen into protein generally has been a relatively minor use of the nitrate undergoing microbially-mediated reactions, and has been more properly termed nitrate assimilation.

Generally when nitrate ion functions as an electron receptor, the product has been NO_2^-. When nitrate ion acts as an electron receptor,

$$\frac{1}{2}NO_3^- + \frac{1}{4}CH_2O = \frac{1}{2}NO_2^- + \frac{1}{4}H_2O + \frac{1}{4}CO_2$$

the free energy yield per electron-mole has been only about 2/3 of the yield when oxygen is the electron receptor. However, nitrate ion is a good electron receptor in the absence of molecular oxygen. One of the factors limiting the use of nitrate ion in this function has been the relatively low concentration of NO_3^- in most waters. Furthermore, nitrite, NO_2^-, has been relatively toxic and tends to inhibit the growth of many bacteria after building up to a certain level. Sodium nitrate has been sometimes used as a "first-aid" treatment in sewage lagoons which have become oxygen-deficient. It provides an emergency source of oxygen to re-establish normal bacterial growth.

4.15 Denitrification

An important special case of nitrate reduction has been denitrification, in which the reduced nitrogen product has been gaseous N_2. At pH 7.00 the free energy change per electron-mole of reaction

$$\frac{1}{5}NO_3^- + \frac{1}{4}CH_2O + \frac{1}{5}H^+ = \frac{1}{10}N_2(g) + \frac{1}{4}CO_2(g) + \frac{7}{20}H_2O \quad (4.1)$$

is -2.84 kcal. The free energy yield per mole of nitrate reduced to N_2 (5 electron-moles) has been higher than that for the reduction of the same quantity of nitrate to nitrite. More important, however, the reduction of a nitrate ion to N_2 gas consumes 5 electrons, compared to only 1 electron for the reduction of NO_3^- to NO_2^-.

Denitrification has been an important process in nature. It is the mechanism by which fixed nitrogen gets returned to the atmosphere. Denitrification is also useful in advanced water treatment for the removal of nutrient nitrogen. The water is treated with a minimum amount of methanol under anaerobic conditions, and N_2 gas is evolved according to the following reaction :

$$5CH_3OH + 6NO_3^- + 6H^+ = 5CO_2 + 3N_2\uparrow + 13H_2O \qquad (4.2)$$

As nitrogen gas is a nontoxic volatile substance which does not inhibit microbial growth, and as nitrate ion is a very efficient electron acceptor, denitrification allows the extensive growth of bacteria under anaerobic conditions.

4.16 The Nitrogen Cycle

The relationships described in the preceding sections on nitrogen transformations of batceria may be summarized in the nitrogen cycle. The nitrogen cycle describes the dynamic processes through which nitrogen gets interchanged among the atmosphere, organic matter, and inorganic nitrogen compounds. It is one of nature's vital dynamic processes. The nitrogen cycle in shown in Fig. 4.5.

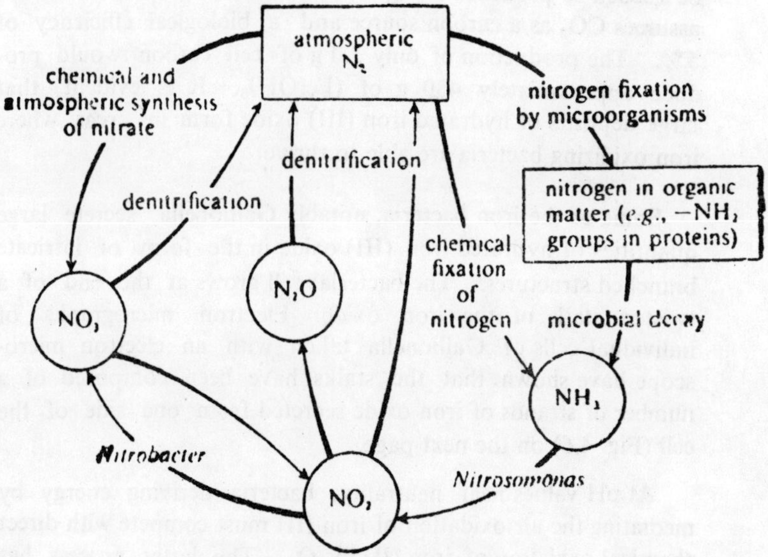

Fig. 4.5. The nitrogen cycle

4.17 Iron and Manganese Bacteria

Some bacteria, including Ferrobacillus, Gallionella and some forms of Sphaerotilus, use iron compounds in getting energy for their matabolic needs. The bacteria are able to catalyze the oxidation of iron (II) to iaon (III) by molecular oxygen :

$$4Fe(II)+4H^{+}+O_2 \rightarrow 4Fe(III)+2H_2O \qquad (4.1)$$

The carbon source for some of these bacteria is CO_2. As they do not need organic matter for carbon, and because they derive energy from the oxidation of inorganic matter, these bacteria may be able to thrive in environments where organic matter is absent.

The microorganism-mediated oxidation of iron (II) has been not a particularly efficient means of energy for metabolic processes. For the reaction

$$FeCO_3+\frac{1}{4}O_2+\frac{3}{2}H_2O=Fe(OH)_3+CO_2 \qquad (4.2)$$

the change in free energy is almost 10 kcal/electron-mole. It has been estimated that approximately 220 g of iron (II) would be needed to produce 1.0 g of cell carbon. The calculation assumes CO_2 as a carbon source and a biological efficiency of 5%. The production of only 1.0 g of cell carbon would produce approximately 430 g of $(Fe(OH)_3$. It is evident that large deposits of hydrated iron (III) oxide form in areas where iron oxidizing bacteria are able to thrive.

Some of the iron bacteria, notably Gallionella, secrete large quantities of hydrated iron (III) oxide in the form of intricate branched structures. The bacterial cell grows at the end of a twisted stalk of the iron oxide. Electron micrographs of individual cells of Gallionella taken with an electron microscope have shown that the stalks have been composed of a number of strands of iron oxide secreted from one side of the cell (Fig. 4.6) on the next page.

At pH values near neutrality, bacteria deriving energy by mediating the air oxidation of iron (II) must compete with direct chemical oxidation of iron (II) by O_2. The latter process has been relatively rapid at pH 7. As a consequence, these bacteria tend to grow in a narrow layer in the region between

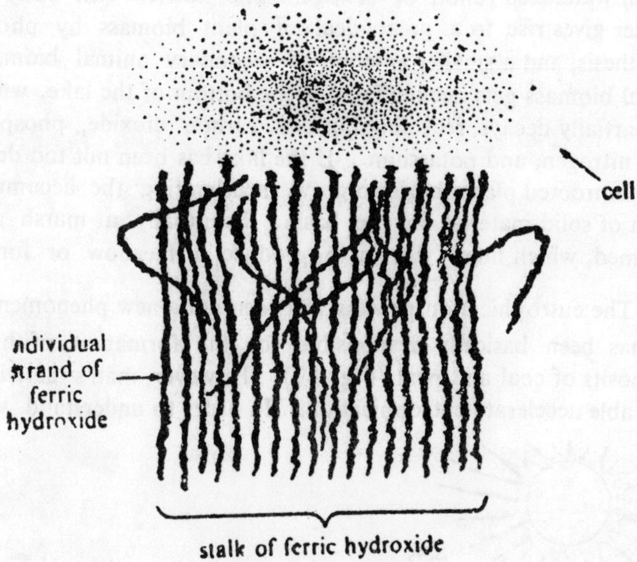

Fig. 4.6. Sketch of a cell of Gallionella showing ferric hydroxide secretion

the oxygen source and the source of iron (II). Hence, iron bacteria are sometimes termed as "gradient organisms," and they grow at intermediate pE values.

Bacteria have been strongly involved in the oceanic manganese cycle. Manganese nodules, a potentially important source of manganese, copper, nickel, and cobalt give rise to different species of bacteria which mediate both the oxidation and reduction of manganese. These reactions are enzymatic in nature and get influenced by seawater cations, especially Ca^{2+} and Mg^{2+}.

4.18 Eutrophication

The term "eutrophication" has been derived from Greek word which means "well nourished." It describes a condition of lakes or reservoirs involving excess algal growth, which may eventually cause their destruction. The first step in eutrophication of a body of water has been an input of nutrients from watershed runoff or sewage. The nutrient-rich body of water gives rise to a great deal of plant biomass by photosynthesis, and a smaller amount of secondary animal biomass. Deal biomass gets accumulated in the bottom of the lake, where it partially decays, recycling nutrient carbon dioxide, phosphorus nitrogen, and potassium. If the lake has been not too deep, bottomrooted plants begin to grow, accelerating the accumulation of solid material in the basin. Eventually a marsh gets formed, which finally fills in to produce a meadow or forest.

The eutrophication process has been not a new phenomenon. It has been basically responsible for the formation of huge deposits of coal and peat (Fig. 4.7). However, man's activities are able accelerate eutrophication. In order to understand why

Fig. 4.7. The eutrophication process, occurring millions of years ago was responsible for the formation of huge deposits of coal and other fossil fuels

this is so, refer to Table 4.2. This table shows the chemical elements needed for plant growth.

Most of these occur at a level which is more than sufficient to upport plant life in the average lake or reservoir. Hydrogen and oxygen are provided by the water itself. Carbon is provided by CO_2 from the atmosphere or from decaying vegetation. Sulfate, magnesium, and calcium normally occur in abundance from mineral strata in contact with the water. The micronutrients are needed at only very low levels (for example,

Table 4.2

Essential Plant Nutrients : Sources and Function

Nutrient	*Source*	*Purpose*
Macronutrients		
carbon (CO_2)	atmosphere, decay	biomass constituent
hydrogen	water	biomass constituent
oxygen	water	biomass constituent
nitrogen (NO_3^-)	decay, atmosphere (nitrogen fixing organisms), pollutants	protein constituent
phosphorus (phosphate)	decay, minerals, pollutants	DNA, RNA constituent
potassium	minerals, pollutants	metabolic function
sulfur (sulfate)	minerals	proteins, enzymes
magnesium	minerals	metabolic function
calcium	minerals	metabolic function
Micronutrients		
B, Cl, Co, Cu. Fe, Mo, Mn, Nai, Si V, Zn	minerals, pollutants	metabolic function and/or constituent of enzymes

approximately 40 ppb for copper). Therefore the nutrients most likely to be limiting have been the "fertilizer" elements : nitrogen, phosphorus, and potassium. These all occur in sewage and are of course found in runoff from heavily fertilized fields. They are also constituents of various kinds of industrial wastes. Each of these elements can come from natural sources – phosphorus and potassium from mineral formations, and nitrogen fixed by bacteria, blue-green algae, or discharge of lightning through the atmosphere.

Generally the plant nutrient most likely to be limiting has been phosphorus, and it has been generally named as the culprit in excessive eutrophication. Household detergents constitute a common source of phosphate in wastewater, and eutrophication control has concentrated upon eliminating phosphates from detergents, removing phosphate at the sewage treatment plant, or preventing phosphate-laden sewage effluents (treated or untreated) from entering bodies of water.

In some cases nitrogen or even carbon constitute limiting nutrients. Particularly in sea water nitrogen may be a limiting nutrient.

The whole eutrophication picture has been a complex one and continued research is required to solve the problem. It is indeed ironic that in a food-poor world, nutrient-rich wastes from over-fertilized fields or sewage are bringing about excessive plant growth in many lakes or reservoirs. This illustrates again that in general there has been no such thing as a pollutant, there have been only resources (in this case plant nutrients) gone to waste.

5

Lithosphere and Soil

5.1 The Origin and Chemical History of the Earth

There are several hypotheses of the origin and chemical history of the Earth. The cold accretion theory seem to be finding greater favor currently than the hot condensation hypothesis. There can account for the low abundances of light gases such as hydrogen, helium krypton and xenon and the appearance of volatile a substance as water. The layered structure of the Earth makes it clear that at least at one point in its early history it was entirely, molten. From the gigantic liquid droplet, the various chemical phases separated out with the heavy iron at the center and a crust of the lighter silicates much like the formation of slak in blast furnance.

It is not, simply a matter of the heavier metals sinking to the center of the Earth and the lighter elements rising to the surface. Contrarly the major phases distribute according to their densities. The distribution of majority of elements is not only determined, by their densities, but also by their solubilities in different phases. Largely on the basis of their distribution in meteorites, the chemical elements can be classified as iron, sulfide, silicate, or gaseous – they are normally found as components of compounds. A number of properties correlate the geochemical nature of the elements *e.g.*, atomic volumes and the heats of formation of the oxides. In addition to liquid-liquid equilibrium solubility criteria, an important factor in determining geochemical behavior is the ease of crystalline lattice substitution, therefore the size, and the outer electronic configuration of an element's ions, is also critical.

The condensation of chemical substances from a cooling of gas suggested that the silicates condense first and metals such as iron, late in the process; therefore a subsequent melting and reversal of phase is necessary to give the Earth the present structure. In order to get the iron at the core the Earth would have to remain molten throughout the accretion period. More recent theories suggest the envision heating by radioactivity which leads to partial or total melting followed by cold accretion of planetesimals and other material. The hot accretion theories say that the Earth's core as forming either during or immediately after the slow accretion process whereas in the cold accretion models the core was formed by subsequent radioactive heating and melting.

The cold Earth model, has given out hypothesis of melting and differentiation. In the layer several hundred kilometers deep the iron of the formerly cold and homogeneous Earth melted to form a large droplet that then slowly sank to the center to form the core and forced the silicates upward. This hypothesis explain that such an unsymmetrical process accounts for the unequal distribution of the, Earth the location of the original protocontinent, in the northern hemisphere in the crustal region. It also explain the "bottomless" Pacific Ocean. The Moon was torn from the Earth and that the Pacific was formed. At Last, as the radioactive heating diminished, the churning Earth quieted down, the mantle film solidified, and the great stable crustal blocks began to take their form.

5.2 Introduction

The crust is the outermost solid layer of the Earth and it contains about 0.4% of the total mass. It is much richer in silicon and oxygen than the Earth as a whole. The crust is heterogeneous, and made up of a large number of very different types of rocks. A rock type may be defined by the minerals it contains and the conditions under which it formed. A mineral is a naturally formed inorganic compound whose composition may be quite complex and may have a fixed crystal lattice, but the atoms, ions or molecular species occupying the lattice positions may differ by greater or lesser amounts from one crystal to the another one.

The following features can infer the conditions of formation of rocks :

(i) The mineral present and is formed under a characteristic range of temperature and pressure.

(ii) The texture of the rock which is determined by the sizes, shapes and inter-relationships of the minerals in the rock.

(iii) The large-scale morphological features. *e.g.* one rock may intrude into another, indicating that it was once molten; or a rock may show ripple marks, indicating that it was deposited as a sediment under water.

The structure and chemical composition of the interior of Earth is determined entirely from seismic measurements, with the help from our chemical analyses of meteorites, heat flow, and gravitational data, and the precession of the equinoxes. Seismic waves from earthquakes are of three types :

(i) primary, longitudinal, small amplitude, compressional P-waves;

(ii) secondary, transverse, larger amplitude, shearing S-waves; and

(iii) large amplitude surface waves. The refraction and absorption of these waves has infessed that the Earth is a complex oval shaped consisting of a solid innermost core surrounded by a liquid core (Fig 5.1). This core material is then covered by a their mantle, the superficial layer of which is called the crust, or together with the upper mantle in more exact terminology the lithosphere proper.

5.3 The Lithosphere

The Earth refers to a cold, spherical, solid planet of the solar system, which spins on its axis and revolves around the sun at a certain constant distance The solid component of Earth is termed as lithosphere. The lithosphere is multilayered and includes following three main layers : crust, mantle and outer and inner core (Fig. 5.1). The core refers to the central fluid or vapourized sphere which is having diameter of about 25`0 km from the centre and is possibly composed of Nickel-Iron. The mantle extends about 29(0 km above the core. This is in a molten state. The crust forms the outermost solid zone of the earth and it is about 8 to 40 km above the mantle. The crust

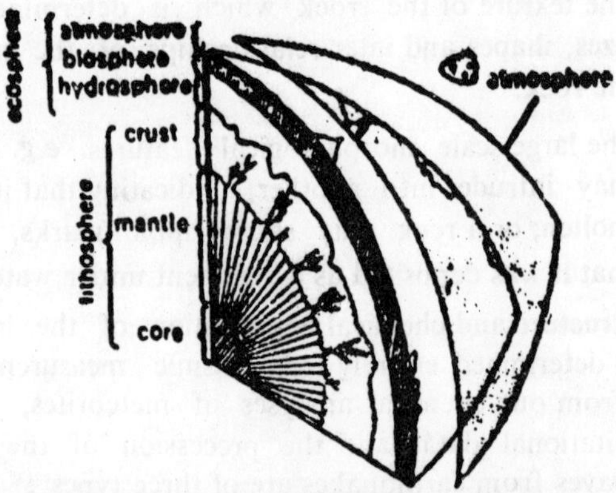

Fig. 5.1. Cross section of the planet showing its different layers

is very complex and its surface is covered with the soil supporting rich and varied biotic communities, for living organisms find in the soil an environmental providing food, shelter, anchorage and concealment from the predators (Wallwork, 197υ).

In terms of the total diameter of the earth, the soil on the earth's surface is only a tissue-thin layer. However, this thin layer of indispensable soil produces the food upon which most living things depend for their existence. In agricultural areas the standard of living is directly related to the quality of soil. Good soil—and a climate conducive to its productivity—is the most valuable asset a nation can have.

5.3.1 The Mantle

The mantle of the Earth accounts for 67% of its total mass and 90% of its total volume. Even though we now have great deal of idea of its elemental composition but the nature of the compounds and phases those are involved remains a subject of considerable controversy.

Seismic measurements have revealed that the structure of the mantle is very complex having lateral heterogeneities as well as a number of well-defined layers. Four different layer are:

(i) the upper mantle (33 to 410 km) with normal S and P seismic velocity gradients.

(ii) a transition region (410 to 1000 km) with greater than normal gradients.

(iii) another normal gradient zone between 1000 and 2700 km forming the first shell of the lower mantle,

(iv) the second shell of the lower mantle (2700 to 2900 km) with gradients near zero.

The chemical composition of the mantle, can be known from extraterrestrial abundances; density, sound velocity, geophysical considerations and experimental studies of phase transitions under high temperature and pressure. Important conclusions can be drawn by determining the composition of the upper mantle, *i.e.* the petrology of ultramafic and basaltic igneous rocks derived from the mantle and brought to the surface by processes such as tectonic movements and the volcanic extrusion of molten magma. The specimens must contain the same level of radioisotopes.

More than 90% by weight of the mantle is contains $FeO-MgO-SiO_2$; $Na_2O - CaO - Al_2O_3$ more than 8%; and no other oxide reaches a concentration of 0.6% in the mantle. Minerology of the mantle can be represented as $CaO\ \ MgO - Al_2O_3-SiO_2$ with FeO substituting for MgO in most magnesium minerals and Na_2O for CaO in plagioclase at low pressures and in jadeitic pyroxene at high pressures.

5.4 The Soil

The soil is one of the most important ecological factor (called edaphic factor) and also is the most characteristic feature of terrestrial environments. It is the loose, friable, unconsolidated top layer of Earth's crust and is the mixture of weathered rock materials (*i.e.*, minerals) and organic detritus, both of which get formed through the physical, chemical and biological processes occurring slowly and slowly for a long period at Earth's surface. Besides being the source for the entry of nutrients and water into plants, the soil is the medium for the detritus food chain : nutrients released in detritus are decomposed by various soil microbes like bacteria. algae, fungi, protozoa, etc., bound in or on soil particles, and taken back into plants through their roots. Soil (mud) is also the main source of nutrients for all aquatic plants (hydrophytes), rooted or submerged or free floating. In addition, soil is the means of support for all terrestrial organisms : plants are anchored to the soil by their root systems; animals walk upon it and are supported by it, as many animals like nematodes, polychates, arachnids, insects, rodents, etc., live under the soil.

The world soil is derived from a Latin word 'solum' which means Earthy material in which plants grow. The science dealing with the study of soil is called soil science, pedology (pedos—Earth) or edaphology (edaphos soil).

A fully developed or mature soil is that state of soil that has assumed the profile features (*i.e.* succession of natural layers), characteristic of predominant soils on the smooth uplands within the general climate and botanic regions in which it is found (Marbut, 1926). According to Dokyachev, (1879), the first soil scientist, the soil is a result of the actions and reciprocal influences of parent rocks, climate topography, plants, animals and age of the land.

Soil is a stratified mixture of inorganic and organic materials, both of which are decomposition products. The mineral constituents of soil are derived from some parent material, the soil forming rocks by fragmentation or weathering, while, organic components of soil are formed either by decomposition (or transformation) of dead remains of plants or animals or through metabolic activities of living organisms present in the soil.

Basically, there are three kinds of soil forming rocks - igneous rocks, sedimentary rocks and metamorphic rocks. The main characteristics of these rocks have been summarized in Table 5.1 on the next page.

The rock cycle is shown in Fig 5 2.

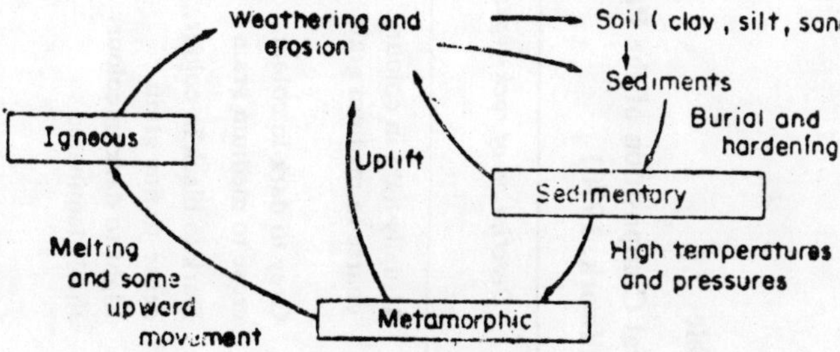

Fig. 5.2. The rock cycle

Soil formation is started by disintegration or wevathering of parent rocks by some physical, chemical and/or biological agents, because of which the soil-forming rocks are broken down in small particles called regoliths. Regoliths are the basic materials which under the influence of various other pedogenic processes finally develop into mature soil.

5.5 Soil Profile Showing Soil Horizons

Typical soils exhibit distinctive layers with increasing depth. (Fig. 5.3). These layers are termed as horizons. The top layer, typically several inches in thickness, is known as the A horizon or topsoil. This is the layer of maximum biological activity in the soil and containg most of the soil organic matter. Metal ions and clay particles in the A horizon are subject to consider-

Table 5.1

Classification, Characteristics and Mineral Composition of the Principal soil-forming rocks (Wallwork, 1970)

Class of rock	*Mode of formation of rock*	*Type*	*Description of rock-types*	*Principal minerals of soil-forming roaks*
A. Igneous rocks	Formed by cooling of molten megma (lava)	1. Granite	Usually light in colour, coarse to medium grain	Quarts, feldspar, mica, amphibole, iron oxides
		2. Diorite	Grey to dark in colour, crose to medium grain	Feldspar, amphibole, iron oxide, biotite
		3. Basalt	Dark to black in colour, dense to fine grain	Feldspar, pyroxene, iron oxide, biotite.
B. Sedimentary rocks	Formed by deposition of weathered minerals which derived from igneous rocks	1. Shales	Light to dark in colour, thinly laminated	Clay minerals, quartz

		2. Sand-stone	Light to red in colour, granular and porous	Quartz, clay minerals, iron oxides, calcium carbonate
		3. Limestone	Light grey, red, brown, or black in colour, fine grained and compact	Calcite, dolomite, iron oxide, clay minerals
C. Meta-morphic rocks	Formed by change of pre-existing rock (*i.e.*, igneous or sedimentary rock) through heat and pressure	1. Gneiss	With light and dark bonds	Much as in granite from which it is formed
		2. Schist	Foliated structure	Much as in basalt or to shale from which it is formed
		3. State	Grey to black in colour, compact and uniform texture	Similar composition to shale from which it is formed
		4. Quart-zite	Light to brown in colour, compact and uniform texture	Similar composition to sand-stone from which it is formed
		5. Marble	Light, red, green or black in colour, compact, fine to coarse texture	Calcite, dolomite formed form lime stone

Fig. 5.3. Soil profile showing soil horizons

able leaching. The next layer is the B horizon, or subsoil. It receives material such as organic matter, salts, or clay particles leached from the topsoil. The C horizon is composed of weathered parent rocks from which the soil originated. These horizons and their subdivisions make up the soil profile shown in Fig. 5.3.

5.6. Chemistry of Minerals of Soil-forming Rocks

Rocks are the chemical mixture of numerous kinds of minerals. The chemical nature of certain most common and abundant minerals of soil forming rocks has been listed in Table 5.2 given on the next page.

Besides these tabulated minerals following minerals occur in low percentage in soil-forming rocks – Toarmative (Boron silicas or Aluminium with alkali metals and Iron and Magnesium), Rutile (Titanium oxides), Zircon (Zirconium oxide), and Gauconite (hydrated silicon of iron and potassium).

Table 5.2

Chemical Composition of some Soil Minerals

Minerals	*Chemical Constituents*
A. Sand and silt minerals	
1 Quartz or silica	SiO_2
2. Feldspars	
(a) Orthoclase	$K_2Al_2Si_6O_{16}$
(b) Plagioclase	$NaAlsi_3O_8$
(c) Calcium feldespar	$CaAl_2Si_2O_8$
3. Micas	
(a) Muscopite	$K(OH)_2Al_2(AlSi_3)O_{10}$
(b) Biotite	K, Mg, Fe, Al silicate
4. Pyroxene	(Mg, Fe) SiO_3
5. Amphibole	$(Mg, Fe)_7 (Si_4O_{11})_2 (OH)_2$
6. Olivine and serpentine	$(Mg, Fe)_2SiO_4$
7. Calcite; magnesite; and dolomite	$CaCO_3$. $MgCO_3$; and $CaCO_3$, $MgCO_3$)
8. Iron oxides	
(a) Haematite	Fe_2O_2
(b) Magnettic	Fe_3O_4
(c) Limonite	FeO (OH), xH_2O
B. Clay minerals	
1. Kaolin	Al_2O_3, $2SiO_2$, $2H_2O$
2. Montmorillonite	(Ca,MgO)Al_2O_3, $5SiO_3$, $5H_2O$

5.7 Major Elements in the Earth's crust

5.7.1 Silicon

Abundance by weight Earth, 14.3%; crust, 29.5%, ocean, 2.9 ppm. The Earth's crust is mainly composed of silicate minerals. The Si O bonds have a large degree of covalent character and is over twice as strong as the Si Si bond therefore the Si - O arrangement is the preferred structure wherever, as in the Earth's crust, there is sufficient oxygen present to allow its formation.

Weathering

The solid rocks those are composing the bulk of the crust do not remain compact and coherent masses when exposed to the air. They are usually covered with a soft particulate layer called soil. Sometimes the solid rocks appear uncovered by soil or other material, but close examination revealed that the surface layers are of different appearance and composition from those of inner layers. Over a period of time, the outer layers are being removed and disintegration of solid rock is taking place by weathering process in which the rocks and minerals are changed until they are chemically and physically in equilibrium with their surroundings.

The mechanism of weathering can be divided into two main steps that operate together and reinforce each other's actions.

(i) Physical, or mechanical, weathering, in which the rock and subsequent fragments are broken into smaller particles and transported from one place to another.

(ii) Chemical weathering, which involves the chemical composition of the rocks and fragments are changing to produce more stable compounds or species.

In the mechanical breakdown of large particles into smaller particles produces a large surface area so that chemical reactions can occur. These changes in chemical composition tend to weaken the structures so that they are easier to break up.

One of the most important features of weathering is that it mobilises many chemical substances. In general the lower the solubility of a compound the smaller will be the interaction between that compound and a living organisms. Hence processes like weathering which affect the solubility of elements are of great importance in controlling the viabi ity of organisms. There is a wide range of quite complex reactions occurring during weathering.

The composition of the parent rock and the weathering conditions control the proportion of soluble and insoluble products formed during weathering. The majority of the minerals in igneous rocks were formed at high temperatures and high pressures. In general the higher the temperature of formation of the mineral, the more rapidly it is likely to undergo weathering. The ionic compounds are the more soluble in water whereas the Si—O bond has more covalent character than the metal – oxygen bonds in minerals. It is found that minerals with isostructural groups and the greatest proportions of silicate units are the most stable, *e.g.*, sodium-rich plagioclases have 61 – 68 % SiO_2 and are much more stable than the calcium-rich plagioclases with 43 – 50% SiO_4.

The isomorphous substitution of one element by another in silicate lattices may cause in stability of the crystal structure. The consequence of this is that the individual crystals of a mineral in a rock can whether at different rates, depending upon the substitution ion of elements. The trace elements released by this weathering can vary to a large extent from rock to rock, even though the mineral composition remains very similar.

The water is a prerequisite for these reactions and in many arid areas the amount of water is so low that phyiscal weathering is the more stronger mechanism. The reactrivity of solutions is increased by the presence of hydrogen ions, which aid the dissolving of metallic elements. The H^+ in water can arise from the following major sources :

(i) Gases dissolved from the atmosphere to water *e.g.* carbon dioxide,

(ii) The oxidation of plant remains which can increase the concentration of carbon dioxide in the soil atmosphere.

(iii) The formation of organic acids by the decay and oxidation of plant remains (Eqn. 5.1).

$$\underset{\text{compound}}{\text{Complex organic}} + O_2 \rightarrow \underset{\text{carboxylic acid}}{RCOOH} + \underset{\text{phenols}}{ArOH} \rightarrow RCOO^- + H^+ + ArO^- + H^+ \qquad (5.1)$$

Reaction of the acidic solution with the silicate minerals reduces the hydrogen ion concentration of the aqueous solution (Eqn. 5.2), and it may even become neutral or alkaline.

$$2H^+(aq) + M_2SiO_4 \longrightarrow H_4MSiO_4 + M^{2+}(aq) \qquad (5.2)$$

These changes in pH may also change the solubility of the compounds present. If the pH is between 5 and 9, silicon is more soluble than aluminium and iron, and will be leached out of a rock or soil to leave behind a mixture of hydrated aluminium and iron oxides ($Al_2O_3nH_2O$ and $Fe_2O_3{\cdot}nH_2O$) which will form a lateritic soil with more aluminium oxide or feralitic soil with more iron oxide. When the pH is less than 5, aluminium becomes more soluble and silicon and will be leached out. The solubility of iron also increases more acidic solutions especially when the ground becomes waterloggged for part of the year and reducing conditions are produced Low pH is usually associated with organic matter, tends to occur close to the surface of a soil or rock. As the acidic water percolates through the soil, reacting with the minerals, the pH of the solution rises and the solubility of iron and aluminium oxides are reduced. The aluminium and iron compounds precipitate out of solution and often form a distinctive layer, known as the B horizon.

The role played by the decay of organic matter in the formation of carbon dioxide and organic acids in soils has which is responsible for lowering the pH and making the soils more acidic, the decay of organic compounds can affect the process of weathering in many other ways. One major effect can be to change the redox conditions. Any such changes bring about changes in the solubility of elements such as iron, sulphur and nitrogen. Many of the organic compounds produced during decomposition can act as complexing agents which may change the solubility of an element. Organic compounds with relatively higher molecular masses, such as those that make up peat and humose layers in soils, are insoluble in water, *e.g.*, lead, forming complexes with these substances are held in immobile forms in surface layers of soils. Compounds with relatively lower molecular masses and those containing hydroxyl or carboxyl groups, are more likely to form soluble complexes with metals and so increase the mobility of the metals. The binding of the organic compound to the metal ion in the complex prevents the metal ion reacting with other compounds. Thus, the chemisty of the complexed ion can be completely different from the chemistry of the simple ion, *e.g.* ion(III) will precipitate from solution when the pH rises above 4. If oxalic acid is present an ion –oxalic-acid complex such as trioxalatoferrate(III), $[Fe(OOCCOO)_3]^3$, is formed that is soluble at pH more than 4.

The interaction of the organic compounds which is produced by microbial action with the minerals in rocks and soils can prove to be the more stronger factor in determining the rate at which weathering proceeds. This is because of the way in which chemical properties as well as solubility can be changed. The complicated chemical reactions which are occuring there is little detailed knowledge of the actual changes.

A characteristic feature of soils is the formation of a series of layers of different composition, called horizons (Fig. 5.3). The thickness, composition and appearance of the various horizons varies largely from place to place, being determined by the interaction of source material, climate, topography, biological activity and age. In general, movement of material is away from the surface and is initially downwards, but may then become lateral with the ground-water flow. Intermediate stages result in the particular types of matter that has comes together in certain horizons, *e.g.*, organic matter in A horizons; ion oxides, clays and co-precipitated trace elements in the B horizon or in the removal of materials from certain horizons, *e.g.*, silicon or aluminium, depending upon pH, from the E horizon.

The general changes that have occured in silicate-based rocks during soil formation and weathering can be understood on following lines.

(i) The breakdown larger particles into smaller particles.

(ii) The formation of new minerals those are having a greater proportion of octahedral structures stable at low temperatures and pressures.

(iii) The preferential loss of silicon, from the tetrahedral units, in comparison to aluminium and iron from the octahedral units.

(iv) The increasing numbers of hydroxyl ion or H_2O groups, compared to oxide ion in the new minerals.

(v) The preferential loss of sodium, calcium and magnesium compared to potassium, aluminium and iron.

(vi) The general mobilisation of trace elements from the original silicate minerals disintegrated through these elements may be trapped once again in the new minerals formed at low temperature.

Both the soluble components and the particulate residues from weathering will be transferred to the oceans. The most important transfer agents are the rivers, glaciers and ground water. Dust particles into the atmosphere may be of considerable importance. The rivers have been estimated to have an average ratio of dissolved-to suspended material of 1 : 2.5, but higher transfer rates and ratios (1 : 4.6) have also been suggested. The actual ratio of dissolved-to-suspended load varies greatly from river to river and even from place to place. Nearly 78% of all suspended material entering the world's oceans comes from South-East Asia. The distribution of the dissolved load entering the oceans is much more evently spread between the continents; whereas Australia and Antarctica provide very low inputs due to their arid and frozen natures respecttvely.

5.7.2 Iron

Abundance by weight : Earth, 34.8%; crust, 5.0%; ocean, 3.4 ppb. As we know that the core is mainly composed of liquid iron and the mantle contains a high percentage of ferromagnesian silicates, both will have higher concentrations of iron then that in the crust. The different oxidation state of the iron which is 0 in the free metal, 2 in ferromagnesian minerals and 3 in many crustal rocks. The oxygen-rich atmosphere of the Earth converts the both iron(0) and iron(II) those are unstable under normal conditions at the Earth's surface, and both are oxidised to iron(III).

The low solubility of iron(III) oxides means that the geochemical cycle of iron (Fig. 5.4) is dominated by solid-transfer

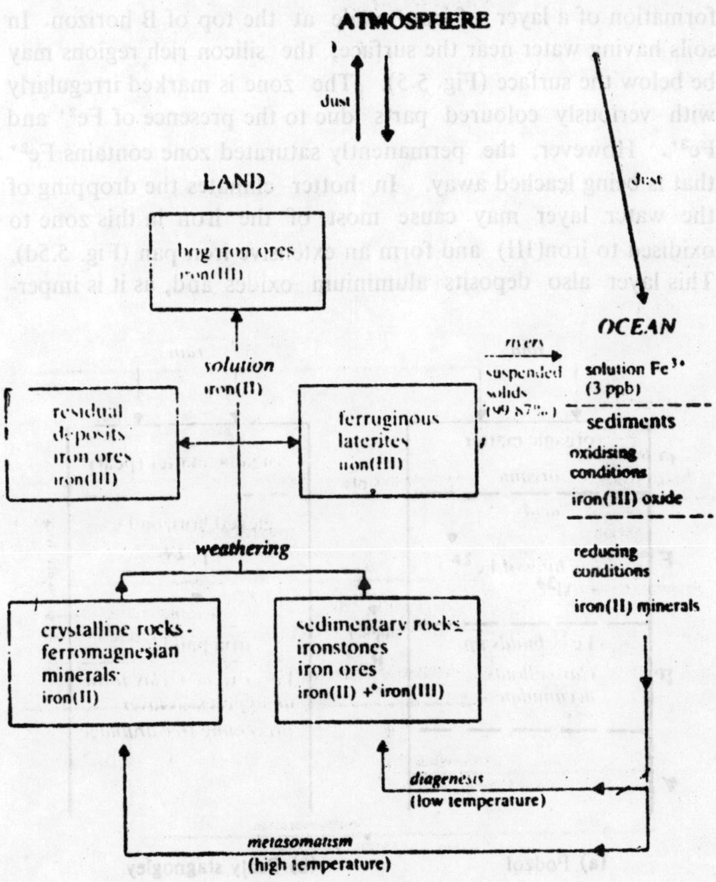

Fig 5.4. The iron cycle

reactions and most of the iron reaching the oceans is carried by rivers as suspended solids.

The stabilities of ferrous and ferric ions are such that only small changes in natural environmental conditions can cause either iron(II) to be oxidised to iron(III) or iron III to be reduced to iron(II). These changes can result in large changes in solubility. Changes in either pH or redox potential (Eh) very important and determines the stability and solubility of ions.

The drying out of the upper layers withtime favours the formation of a layer of iron oxide at the top of B horizon. In soils having water near the surface, the silicon rich regions may be below the surface (Fig. 5.5). The zone is marked irregularly with veriously coloured parts due to the presence of Fe^{2+} and Fe^{3+}. However, the permanently saturated zone contains Fe^{2+} that is being leached away. In hotter climates the dropping of the water layer may cause most of the iron in this zone to oxidised to iron(III) and form an extensive iron pan (Fig. 5.5d). This layer also deposits aluminium oxides and, as it is imper-

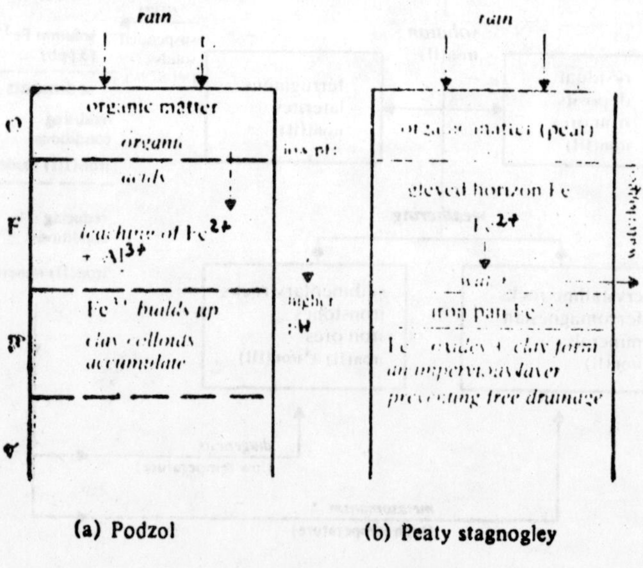

(a) Podzol (b) Peaty stagnogley

vious, subsequent heavy rainfall tends to wash off the loosely held soil leaving the hard lateritic layer exposed.

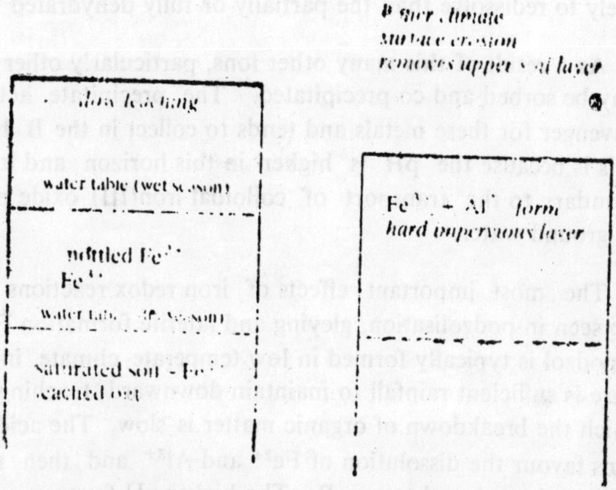

(c) Groundwater gley (d) Laterite

Fig. 5.5. The formation of podzolic, gleyed and lateritic soils

In natural systems there are many different dissolved species other than iron which can influence the behaviour of iron by reacting with it to form either relatively insoluble compuunds *e.g.* sulphide or phosphate or stable complexes *e.g.* organic acids with iron (III) that prevent the iron being precipitated. It can be seen that haemetite (Fe_2O_3), siderite ($FeCO_3$), pyrites (FeS_2) and soluble Fe^{2+} are all possible phases that can exist in soil. The most common iron species are ferrous ions in acidic and reducing conditions and haemetite in alkaline oxidising conditions. The haemetite is the most stable oxide, goethite (FeO.OH) and other hydrated oxides are almost as stable and just as insoluble. The conversion from one of these hydrated solids, which may be precipitated first to haemetite occurs at very slow rate. It is often found that haemetite is formed in warm wet regions.

As the boundary between the Fe^{2+} and Fe_2O_3 domains is just on the acid, reducing side of normal surface waters, small changes in pH or Eh may result in either marked dissolution or precipitation of iron. Firstly, gelatinous hydrated iron(III) oxide,

$Fe_2O_3 \cdot nH_2O$ is precipitated which gradually dehydrates on ageing, though formation of Fe_2O_3 may take years. The freshly precipitated and highly hydrated form of the iron(III) is more likely to redissolve than the partially or fully dehydrated form.

As a result of this many other ions, particularly other metals, may be sorbed and co-precipitated. The precipitate acts as a scavenger for these metals and tends to collect in the B horizon. This is because the pH is higher in this horizon and it acts as boundary to the transport of colloidal iron(III) oxide particles by ground water.

The most important effects of iron redox reactions in soils are seen in podzolisation, gleying and laterite formation Fig. 5.5. A podzol is typically formed in low temperate climate in which there is sufficient rainfall to maintain downward teaching and in which the breakdown of organic matter is slow. The acid conditions favour the dissolution of Fe^{2+} and Al^{3+} and then transfer from horizon A to horizon B. The higher pH favours precipitation of iron(III) oxide, together with the deposition of clay and other colloids.

The amount of iron in the biosphere is much less than in the lithosphere, but it is essential to the functioning of all organisms. As we know that iron is a common constituent of soils, levels in solution are generally low and it is not very available. One of the important functions of iron is to act as an oxygen carrier in vertebrates. Oxygen is carried to the cells of the body by haemoglobin molecules concentrated in the red blood cells. The cells of the body contain myoglobin, which accepts and stores the oxygen carried by the haemoglobin. Both haemoglobin and myoglobin contain iron(II) bound to the four pyrrole nitrogen atoms of protoporphyrin ring system.

Iron is the most commonly used metal, with iron production more than 600 million tonnes per annum and steel production more than 700 million tonnes per annum.

Iron is produced by the reduction of various ores like haemetite, Fe_2O_3; goethite, FeOOH; magnetite, Fe_3O_4; siderite, $FeCO_3$.

One of the reasons that why iron has been used by man for so long is that its reduction to form metal is fairly easly using carbon and associated compounds.

$$2Fe_2O_3 + 3C \longrightarrow 4Fe + 3CO_2 \tag{5.3}$$

Iron is unstable under the conditions existing on the Earth's surface. Which can be exhibited by the formation of rust, *i.e.*, a hydrated iron(III) oxide of variable composition, which is the best known example of corrosion– the deterioration of a substance by environmental constituents.

The corrosion process involves the loss of one or more electrons as the corroding metal is oxidised *i.e.* for corrosion to occur there must be an electron acceptor usually oxygen.

$$M \longrightarrow M^{2+} + 2e^- \xrightarrow{O} O^{2-} \xrightarrow{M^{2+}} MO \tag{5.4}$$

The presence of water usually increases the rate and extent of corrosion which can be understood on the basis of following steps.

(i) It can provide electron acceptors in either acid or alkaline solutions :

$$M \longrightarrow M^{2+} + 2e^- \xrightarrow{2H^+} H_2 \tag{5.5}$$

$$2M \longrightarrow 2M^{2+} + 4e^- \xrightarrow{O_2 + 2H_2O} 4OH^- \tag{5.6}$$

(ii) It can provide an electron-transfer pathway, if it contains dissolved ions (*e.g.* sea water.)

(iii) It can remove reaction products that could inhibit further reaction by building up a protective coating, if it contains dissolved ions that can form soluble complexes with the metal ions, *e.g.* $[FeCl_4]^-$;

(iv) It can modify the structure of the reaction products so that they provide less inhibition to corrosion–*e.g.* rust is hydrated iron(III) oxide, $Fe_2O_3 \cdot nH_2O$, whose volume is much greater than that of metallic iron : rust forms a loose, porous coating, whereas in the absence of water Fe_2O_3 will form a coherent, non-porous protective layer because its volume and crystal structure are much closer to that of metallic iron.

5.7.3 Aluminium

Abundance by weight : Earth, 1.8%; crust, 8.2%; ocean, 1ppb.

Aluminium is the third most abundant element in the Earth's crust, and, is widely dispersed in silicate minerals. In the cases such as feldspars and clays in which the aluminium forms an essential structural component they an known as alumino-silicates. In minerals such as pyroxenes and amphiboles, the aluminium is only present as an isomorphous substituent for varying proportions of silicon though its presence is not essential for the stability of the crystal structure. The larger size of the aluminium in comparison to silicon allows it to form stable octahedral structures with oxide ions, $[AlO_6]$, as well as tetrahedral units.

The proportion of aluminium in weathered material gradually increases as weathering proceeds. As the solubility of aluminium is lower than that of silicon in the pH range 4.5-9.5. The changes occurring during weathering follow the order as shown in Fig. 5.6, unless acid conditions prevail. The proportion of aluminium in the soil can be used to indicate either how intensely or for how long weathering has continued. The formation of iron oxides will also occur at a pH greater than 4,5, unless reducing conditions, due to waterlogging aid their removal. In tropical climates weathering to form insoluble layers of

weathering increases
——————————→

aluminium in three-dimensional aluminosilicates *e.g.* feldspars	clays: 2 : 1 clays	clays: 1 : 1 clays	aluminium oxides *e.g.* gibbsite
$NaAlSi_3O_4$	$Al_4(Si_4O_{10})_2(OH)_4$	$Al_4Si_4O_{10}(OH)_8$	$Al_2O_3\text{-}3H_2O$
Si/Al 3/1	2/1	1/1	0/1

iron in silicates ———→ goethite FeO.OH or haematite Fe_2O_3

Fig. 5.6. Chemical changes due to weathering process

aluminium and iron oxides may be very fast. If it is large enough, the aluminium-rich bauxite deposits can be used as the starting material for the production of aluminium.

The aluminosilicates and the hydrated oxide are both particularly stable, however the metal is even less stable than metallic iron under the conditions existing at the Earth's surface. Therefore the production of pure aluminium is a very energy consuming process that follows a quite different route from that taken in producing iron and steel.

The Ore of aluminium is known as Bauxite which on treatment with sodium hydroxide gives pure alumina (Al_2O_3).

Soluble Aluminium Ions

The presence of aluminium species in solution appears to play a part in controlling the pH of acid soil waters in the range pH 3-6 (Fig. 5.7). Increasing inputs of acid, either from acid rainfall or from decaying organic matter from forestry, will result in increasing removal of aluminium from soils that have a low

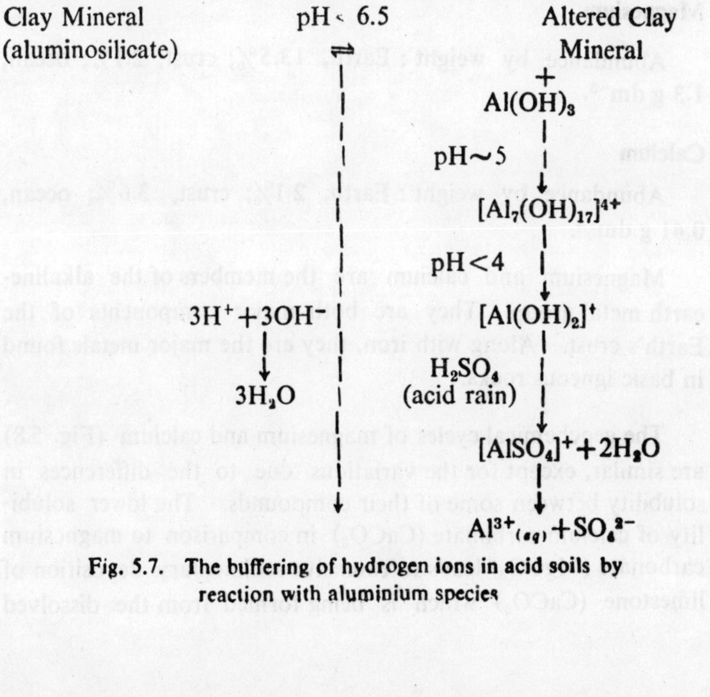

Fig. 5.7. The buffering of hydrogen ions in acid soils by reaction with aluminium species

buffering capacity. Soluble aluminium is moderately toxic to most plants effects of acidification of soils is to remove the concentration of some essential elements and increase the concentration of toxic elements. It can be suggested that there are mainly three phases in the effects of acid rain on forested areas.

(i) The trees gets benefit from the increased sulphur and nitrogen added to the soils.

(ii) Continued acidification reduces the soil's neutralising, or buffering, capacity and leaches out soluble metallic nutrients such as calcium and magnesium.

(iii) The process accelerates and aluminium is extracted from the soil minerals, making the soil toxic to the trees. At the same time heavy metals which also toxic, are mobilised. The critical pH appears to be nearly 4.3, with aluminium as the destructor below this value.

5.7.4 Magnesium and Calcium

Magnesium

Abundance by weight : Earth, 13.5%; crust, 2.1%; ocean, 1.3 g dm^{-3}.

Calcium

Abundance by weight : Earth, 2 1%; crust, 3.6%; ocean, 0.41 g dm^{-3}.

Magnesium and calcium are the members of the alkaline-earth metal group. They are both major components of the Earth's crust. Along with iron, they are the major metals found in basic igneous rocks.

The geochemical cycles of magnesium and calcium (Fig. 5.8) are similar, except for the variations due to the differences in solubility between some of their compounds. The lower solubility of calcium carbonate ($CaCO_3$) in comparison to magnesium carbonate ($MgCO_3$) leads to extensive sedimentary deposition of limestone ($CaCO_3$) which is being formed from the dissolved calcium which has been transported by rivers into the ocean. Some magnesium was incorporated in these limestone deposits as they were also precipitated. In addition, dolomite ($CaCO_3 \cdot MgCO_3$) may be formed as a mineral in its own way. Both calcium, as the sulphates anhydrite ($CaSO_4$) and gypsum ($CaSO_4.2H_2O$), and magnesium, as the chloride ($MgCl_2.6H_2O$) and as sulphate ($MgSO_4$) are found in evaporite deposits.

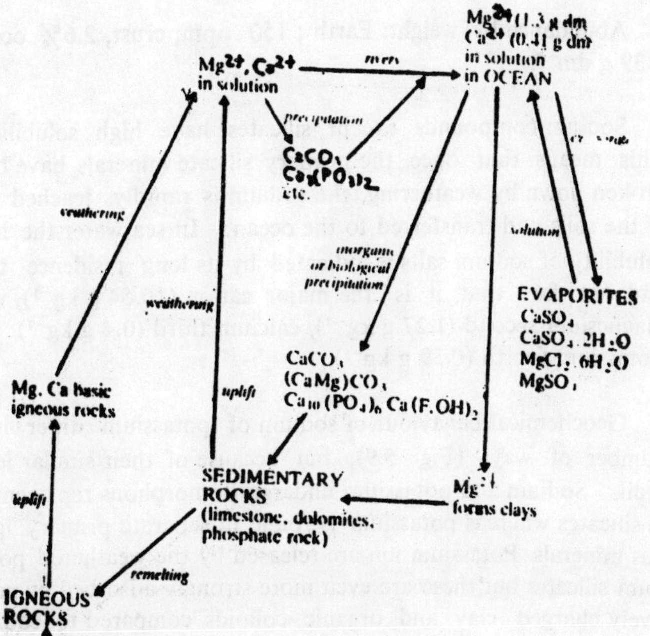

Fig. 5.8. Geochemical cycles of magnesium and calcium

The lower solubility of the calcium sulphates lead to their formation. These precipitation processes favour the precipitation of calcium in preference to magnesium from sea water. There is a marked reduction in the proportion of calcium relative to magnesium in sea water ($Ca^{2+} = 1.2\%$ dissolved solids; $Mg^{2+} = 3.7\%$ dissolved solids) compared with river water ($Ca^{2+} = 20\%$ and $Mg^{2+} = 3.4\%$ of dissolved solids).

5.7.5 Sodium and Potassium

Sodium

Abundance by weight : Earth; 0.3%; crust, 2.8% ocean, 1.05%.

Potassium

Abundance by weight: Earth ; 150 ppm; crust, 2.6% ocean, 0.39 g dm^{-3}.

Sodium compounds except silicates have high solubilities. This means that once the primary silicate minerals have been broken down by weathering, the sodium is rapidly leached out of the soils and transferred to the ocean. In sea water the high solubility of sodium salts is indicated by its long residence time and the fact that it is the major cation (10.54 g kg^{-1}), with magnesium second (1.27 g kg^{-1}), calcium third (0.4 g kg^{-1}) and potassium fourth (0.39 g kg^{-1}).

Geochemical behaviour of sodium of potassium differ in a number of ways (Fig. 5.9), but because of their similar ionic radii. Sodium and potassium undergo isomorphous replacement in silicates whereas potassium is found in separate primary igneous minerals. Potassium ion are released by the weathered potassium silicates but these are even more strongly adsorbed by negatively charged clay and organic colloids compared to sodium ions. Unlike sodium, the potassium is again readily incorporated into silicate structures with the formation of clay minerals and its concentration in biological material is about fifteen times higher compared to that of sodium. As a result the concentration of potassium in fresh water is about one-third that of sodium and the residence time of potassium in the ocean is ten million years.

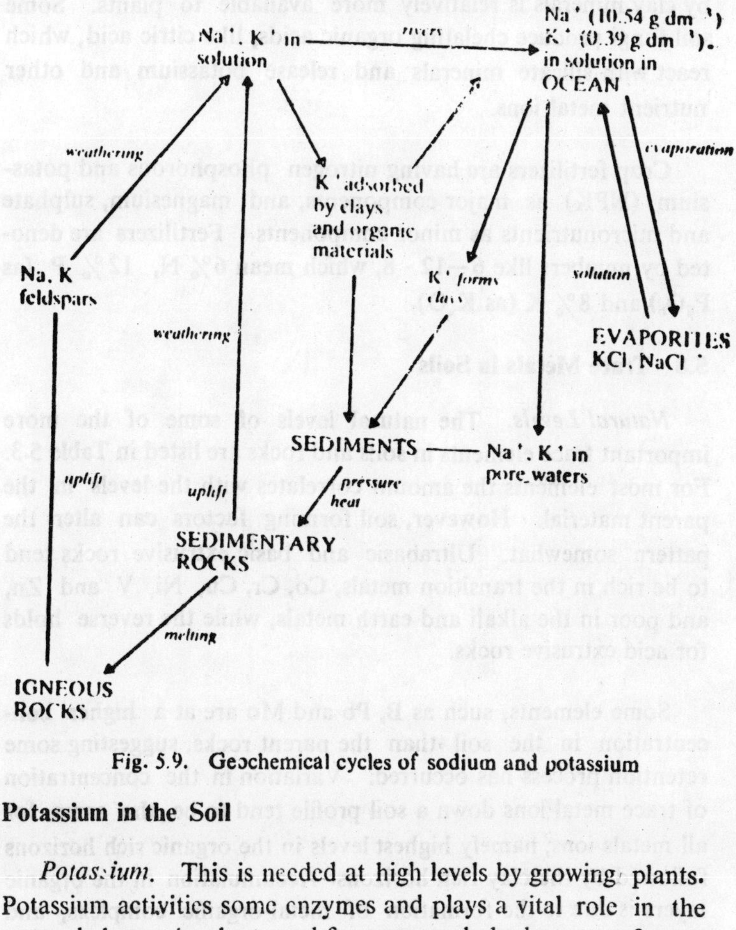

Fig. 5.9. Geochemical cycles of sodium and potassium

Potassium in the Soil

Potassium. This is needed at high levels by growing plants. Potassium activities some enzymes and plays a vital role in the water balance in plants and for some carbohydrate transformations. Crop yields are generally greatly reduced in potassium deficient soils.

Potassium is one of the most abundant elements in the earth's crust, occurring to the extent of 2.6%, but much of this potassium is not easily available to plants. An example is some silicate minerals such as leucite, $K_2O.Al_2O_3.4SiO_2$, which contain strongly bound potassium. Exchangeable potassium held by clay minerals is relatively more available to plants. Some soil fungi produce chelating organic acids, like citric acid, which react with silicate minerals and release potassium and other nutrient metal ions.

Crop fertilizers are having nitrogen phosphorous and potassium (NPK) as major components, and magnesium, sulphate and micronutrients as minor components. Fertilizers are denoted by numbers llke 6—12 - 8, which mean 6% N, 12% P (as P_2O_5) and 8% K (as K_2O).

5.8 Trace Metals in Soils

Natural Levels. The natural levels of some of the more important trace elements in soils and rocks are listed in Table 5.3. For most elements the amount correlates with the levels in the parent material. However, soil forming factors can alter the pattern somewhat. Ultrabasic and basic extrusive rocks tend to be rich in the transition metals, Co, Cr, Cu, Ni, V and Zn, and poor in the alkali and earth metals, while the reverse holds for acid extrusive rocks.

Some elements, such as B, Pb and Mo are at a higher concentration in the soil than the parent rocks, suggesting some retention process has occurred. Variation in the concentration of trace metal ions down a soil profile tend to be the same for all metals ions; namely highest levels in the organic rich horizons followed by the clay rich horizons. Accumulation in the organic layers is due to the formation of metal-organic complexs, and in the clay zones due to sorption. In some tropical soils the major accumulation is in the clay-rich horizons, because of limited organic material. Titanium generally increases down a soil profile. Sandy soils are normally deficient in trace elements because of poor retention.

In acid soils the common form of most trace metals is the hydrated cation, which are soluble, and relatively easily leached, while at higher pH insoluble carbonates, oxides and hydroxides form, so the metals are retained. In semi-arid to arid soils

Table 5.3

Some Trace Elements in Soils

Element	*Crustal abundance ppm*	*Basic Rocks ppm*	*Acid Rocks ppm*	*Sedimentary Rocks ppm*	*Range in Soils ppm*	*Approximate Mean in soils ppm*
1	2	3	4	5	6	7
As	2	1.5	1.5	12	1-100	1
B	10	1-2	3	100	tr*-300	20-50
Co	25	50	8	20	0.05-300	10-15
Cr	100	2000	2	100-500	tr-4000	100-300
Cu	55	150	10	10-100	tr-300	15-40
Fe	50,000	100,000	25,000	35,000	2-50%	30,000

(Contd.)

1	2	3	4	5	6	7
Mn	1000	2000	1000	1000	tr-10,000	500-1000
Mo	1.5	2	2.5	2	tr-24	1-2
Ni	80	220-,000	10	52	tr-5000	20-30
Pb	16	3	24	19	tr-1200	15-25
Se	0.05	0.1	0.1	0.4	tr-12	0.01
Ti	5600	9000	2300	3800	tr-25,000	4000-5000
V	135	200	50	100	tr-400	100
Zn	70	100	60	95	tr-900	50-100

*tr=trace

(vertisols) with high pH trace metal levels may be high. In podsols (leached soils) levels will tend to be lower.

The available trace metal in a soil is not normally the same as the total concentration, but is the amount extracted by different reagents, such as water, ammonium acetate, oxalic acid, ammonium oxalate, mineral acids and EDTA. Depending on the reagent the amount extracted is said to be an estimate of what is available to plants. Extraction studies suggest that leached soils (*e.g.*, podsols) high organic soils (*e.g.*, peats), sandy soils, leached acid soils, and alkaline soils can be deficient in available trace metals. For example copper levels may be quite high in peaty soils, but unavailable to plants because of stable complexes formed with organic acids.

The availability of selenium is important as it is an essential element for animals (and may be man). The levels in rocks range from 0.05 ppm in granites to 0.6 ppm in shales with a mean around 0.1 ppm. Selenium is often found associated with sulphur around volcanic areas and in rocks and minerals. But selenium species are less readily oxidised and are less mobile than sulphur, so it is not as readily removed by weathering. The differences in the redox chemistry of S and Se helps to explain their different chemistry in soil.

$$H_2S \rightarrow S+2H^++2e, \; -E_0=-0.14\ V, \qquad (5.1)$$

$$H_2Se \rightarrow Se+2H^++2e, \; -E_0+0.40\ V, \qquad (5.2)$$

$$S+3H_2O \rightarrow H_2SO_3+4H^+=4e, -E_0=-0.45\ V, \qquad (5.3)$$

$$Se=3H_2O \rightarrow H_2SeO_3+4H^++4e, -E_0=-0.74\ V, \qquad (5.4)$$

$$H_2SO_3+H_2O \rightarrow SO_4^{2-}+4H^++2e, \; -E_0=-0.17\ V, \qquad (5.5)$$

$$H_2SeO_3+H_2O \rightarrow SeO_4^{2-}+4H^++2e-E_0=-1.15\ V. \qquad (5.6)$$

Relative to sulphur, elemental selenium is the more redox stable element, and for the oxyanions selenite is the favoured form for Se, while sulphate is the favoured form for S. From the selenium E_h—pH diagram, Fig. 5.10, it can be seen that the dominant selenium species is selenite in acid scils. At higher pH, since the oxidation potential of equation (6) is less negative the product, SeO_4^{2-}, become more important. The selenite ion in iron rich soils forms insoluble basic fersic selenite, or sorbs strongly on to iron oxides. This shows up in the acid soils of Hawaii where the selenium content can be as high as 20 ppm and yet very little is available to plants. In alkaline soils, even with low Se levels, plants, especially accumulator plants (*e.g.*, species of Astragalus) can attain high levels of Se, because more soluble SeO_4^{2-} is the common form in the soil. An Australian study has found an inverse relationship between the selenium content of plants and rainfall. In high rainfall areas, where acid soils occur, the Se levels in plants are low (< 0.1 ppm), whereas the reverse holds in low rainfall areas (plant Se ~0.7 ppm, yearly rainfall <250.mm).

Iron and manganese, which are relatively abundant in soils can influence the distribution of trace metals. Iron occurs, either as a replacement for All in clays, or as oxides and hydroxide minerals, *e.g.*, goethite, $\alpha FeO(OH)$; hematite, αFe_2O_3 (the main two); maghemite, γFe_2O_3; and lepidocrocite, $\gamma FeO(OH)$. Manganese also occurs as oxides, but more complex, *e.g.*, lithiophorite, $Li_2Mn_2Al_8Mn_{10}O_{35}14H_2O$ and birnessite (Na, Ca) Mn_7O_{14} $2.3H_2O$. Manganese oxides tend to concentrate Fe, CO, Ni, Cu,.Zn, Ba and Pb while iron oxides concentrate V, Mn, Ni, Cu,Zn, As, Se, MO, P, S, Si. The last six elements associated with iron, occur as oxyanions, therefore, iron oxides appear to have greater attraction for oxyanions, than Mn oxides. To some extent the availability of these trace elements is controlled by the availability of iron and manganese in the soils. The tendency of Mn and Fe oxides to concentrate trace metals can be explained in terms of isomorphous replacement of ions. However, lattice energies, and may be crystal field stabilization energies, will contribute to the overall stabilization of the replacement process.

Some of the important element have been discussed in detail in the following sections.

5.8.1 Lead

Abundance by weight: crust, 13 ppm; ocean, 0.03 ppb.

The geochemical cycle of lead (Fig. 5.10), show that the rate of extraction is about ten times greater than the natural rate of weathering.

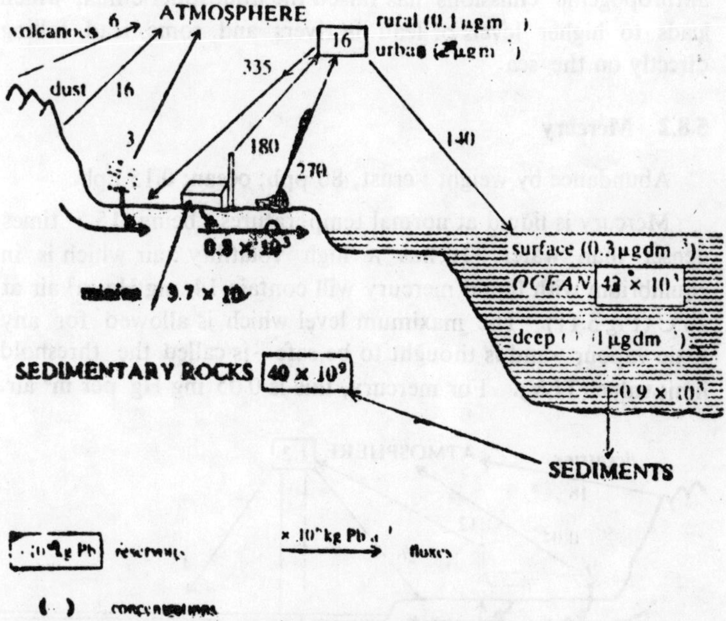

Fig 5.10. The lead cycle

Lead ores can be quite rich in lead, the cut-off grade is about 20% but the average lead concentration in rocks 13 mg/kg and in soils it is 20 mg/kg which is low.

Lead sulphide is associated with black shales. The insoluble sulphides of metals such as lead, copper and mercury were precipitated when these lead sulphide has a low solubility fine-grained lead sulphide marine deposits formed under reducing conditions in which sulphate was reduced to sulphide (10^{-27} mol/liter) but the other lead compounds solubility is usually less than 10^{-6} mol/liter. The weathering of lead ores usuatly produces immobile compounds, with low concentrations of lead in natural waters. The majority of lead in rocks and is present in the form of silicate structure which substitutes the element like calcium. In soils the lead tends to be held strongly by organic matter. About 95% of the lead being transferred to the oceans by rivers was transported as suspended sediment (inorganic and organic). The increase in aerial dispersion from anthropogenic emissions has raised the atmospheric flux, which leads to higher levels of lead in rivers and some lead falling directly on the sea.

5.8.2 Mercury

Abundance by weight : crust, 80 ppb; ocean; 0.15 ppb.

Mercury is liquid at normal temperatures, being 15.5 times denser than water. It has a high volatility : air which is in equilibrium with liquid mercury will contain 14 mg Hg m^3 air at 20°C (Fig 5.11). The maximum level which is allowed for any toxic vapour – and is thought to be safe – is called the threshold limit value (TLV). For mercury, this is 0.05 mg Hg per m^3 air.

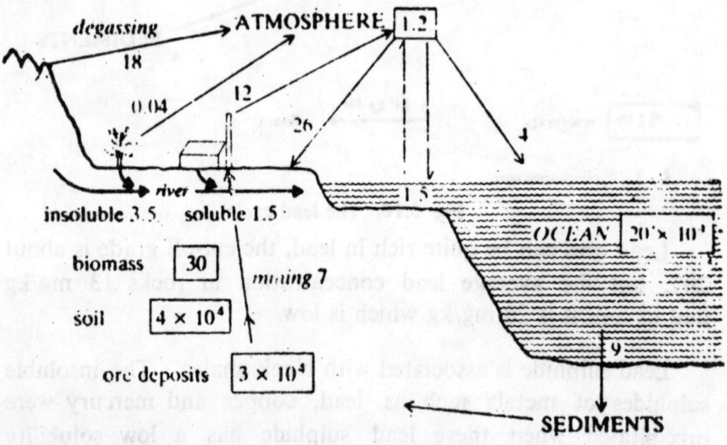

Fig. 5.11. The mercury cycle

As mercury is associated with lead-zinc-silver ores, the presence of high levels of mercury vapour in the atmosphere, or in the air trapped in soil, may be used to show the existance of these ore bodies. Most of the mercury compounds are comparatively volatile; even mercuric sulphide, HgS, which is the major mercury ore mineral, cinnabar, gives 10 ng Hg m^3 in dry air.

The Geochemical cycle of mercury is shown in Fig.

5.8.3 Zinc and Cadmium

Zinc

Abundance by weight : crust, 70 ppm; ocean, 11 ppb.

Cadmium

Abundance by weight : crust, 0.2 ppm; ocean, 0.11 ppb.

The cycles of zinc and cadmium (Fig. 5.12) are very much related to each other as natural zinc minerals contain small amounts of cadmium. Zinc, cadmium and mercury are the members of the same group in the periodic table, however, the inner electron arrangement of mercury differs from that of zinc and cadmium. The hydrated zinc ion ($Zn^{2+}_{(aq)}$) is comparatively more stable than the hydrated cadmium ion ($Cd^{2+}_{(aq)}$). As a

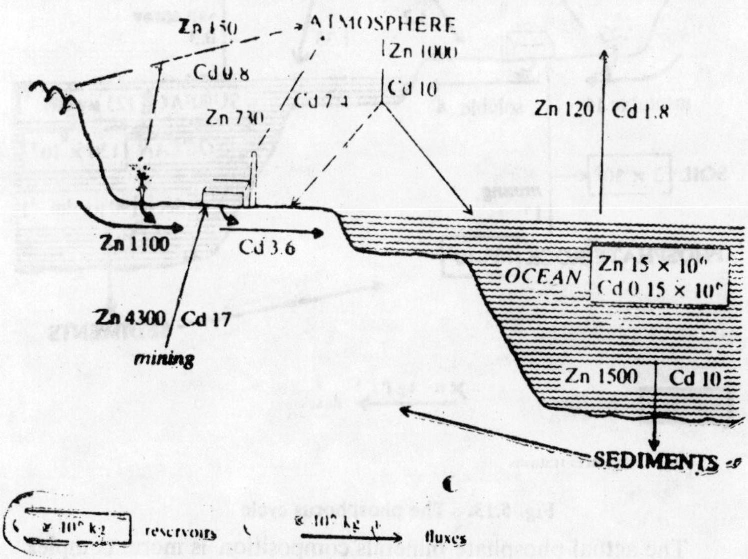

Fig. 5.12. The zinc and cadmium cycles

result, when there is competition to bind to sites in insoluble species, cadmium tends to bind more strongly than zinc, particularly if a metal-sulphur bond is formed. Therefore zinc is displaced by cadmium in many zinc containing enzymes.

5.8.4 Phosphorus

Abundance by weight : Earth, 0.2%; crust, 1050 ppm; ocean, 88 ppb.

The solubility and volatility is low for naturally occurring phosphorus compounds that is why the geochemical fluxes of the element are mainly dependent upon suspended-solid (Fig. 5.13). The phosphorus exists as the orthophosphate group, PO_4^{3-}, bound to a cation in insoluble, inorganic compounds or as a component of organic molecules.

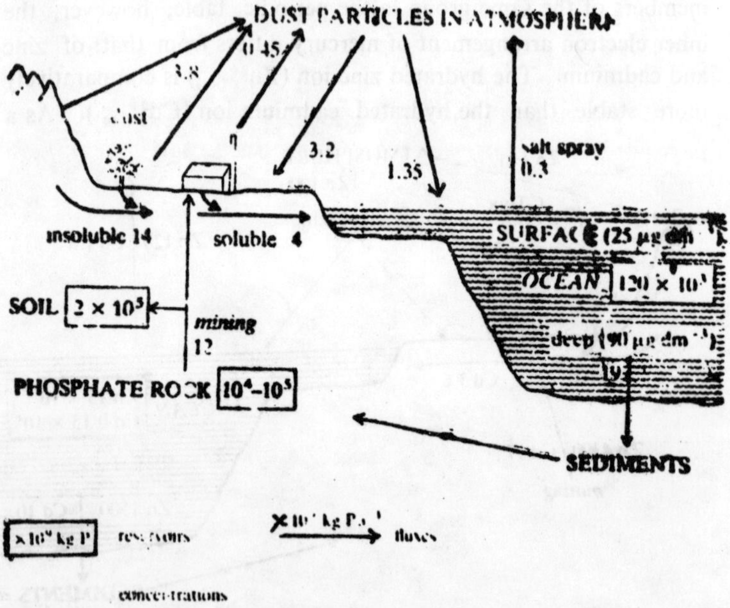

Fig. 5.13. The phosphorus cycle

The actual phosphate minerals composition is more complex than the formulae given, with a high degree of isomorphous substitution between the major cations Ca^{2+}, Al^{3+}, Fe^{2+} and Fe^{3+}, and the incorporation of comparatively large quantities of trace elements.

Phosphorus is an essential constituent of the genetic and information-carrying molecules DNA, RNA and of the energy-transferring molecules ATP, ADP and AMP. This confirms that phosphorus is an essential element for all living organisms and oftenly a limiting factor in the fertility of soils and aquatic eco-systems. Its availability as a nutrient is limited due to the low solubility of the inorganic compounds.

By cellular metabolism or the action of phosphatizing bacteria to dissolved phosphates breaks down the phosphorus in the protoplasm of plants and animals (Fig. 5.14). These dissolved

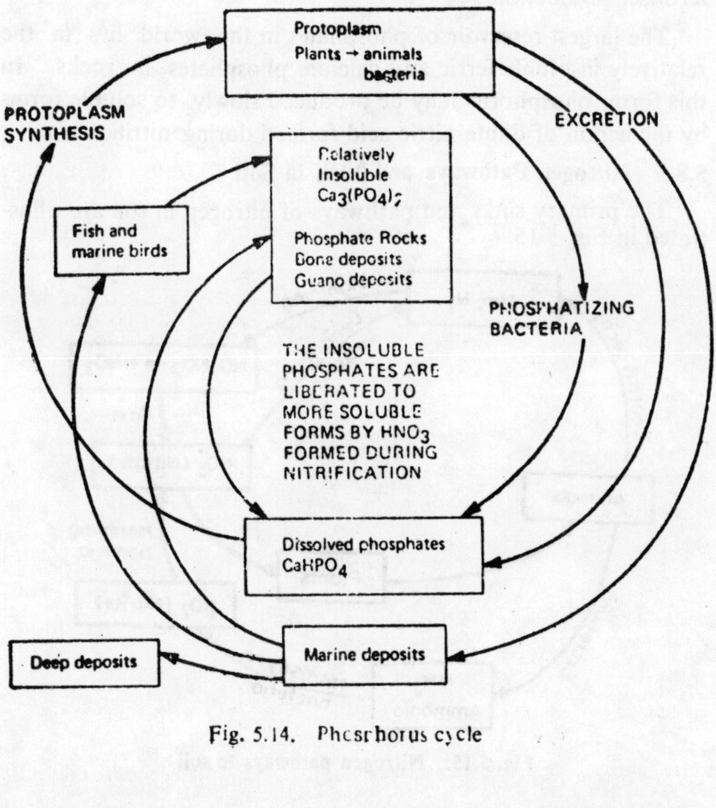

Fig. 5.14. Phosphorus cycle

phosphates can be used directly in protein synthesis in plants as primary nutrients, or they may enter marine deposits and become fixed in relatively insoluble forms of phosphate rocks, $Ca_3(PO_4)_2$. Phosphates may be locked up for considerable periods of time by grows and bone until artificially recovered in bone meal and mining. In general, the loss of phosphorus to the ocean has been higher compared to the gain to land, and this has become a practical problem in several countries like India, where there is a shortage of artificial fertilizers. By burning animal wastes instead of using them as natural fertilizer. India has also mistreated and defeated natural ecosystem principles. Cow dung is dried and is utilized as a important fuel source—a process which has short-circuited natural nitrogen and phosphorus cycles and thus robbed the soil of basic nutrients. Now this is being get right by an expensive program of artificial fertilizer production.

The largest reservoir of phosphates in the world lies in the relatively insoluble ferric and calcium phosphates in rocks. In this form, phosphorus may be produced slowly to soluble forms by the action of dilute nitric acid formed during nitrification.

5.8.5 Nitrogen Pathways and NPK in Soil

The primary sinks and pathways of nitrogen in soil are illustrated in Fig. 5.15.

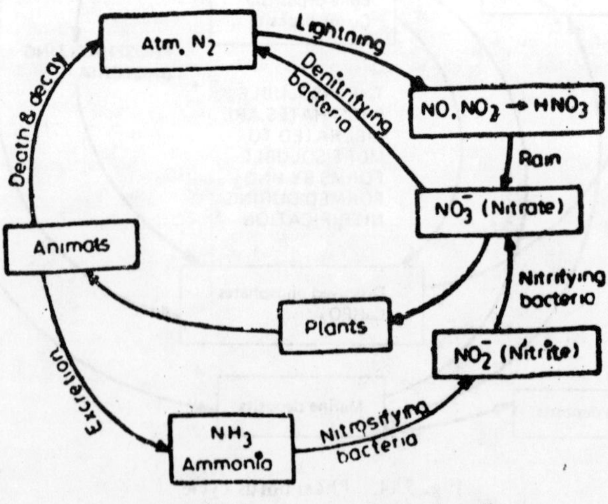

Fig. 5.15. Nitrogen pathways in soil

The nitrogen content in soil has been mostly of organic nature (90%) which gets resulted from the decay of dead plants (biomass) and animals, plant residues and faeces, urine of animals, etc. It gets hydrolyzed to NH_4^+, which can get oxidized to NO_3^- by natural processes in soil. Nitrogen bound to soil humus has been responsible for maintaining soil fertility.

Plants NO_3^- from soil in general. When nitrogen is applied to soils as NH_4^+ (fertilizer), nitrifying bacteria are able to convert it into NO_3^- for use by plants. Certain leguminous plants, *e g.*, soybeans, alfalfa, clover, etc., have the unique ability to fix atmospheric nitrogen through nitrogen fixing bacteria on their root nodules. Legumes can add huge quantities of nitrogen to soil.

5.8.6 Phosphorous in Soil

Although the percentage of phosphorous in plant material has been somewhat relatively low, it is an essential component of plants. Phosphorus, like nitrogen, must be present in a simple inorganic form before it can be taken up by plants. In the case of phosphorus the utilizable species is some form of orthophosphate ion. In the pH range predominant in most soils, $H_2PO_4^-$ and HPO_4^{2-} are the predominant orthophosphate species which are utilised by plants.

In relatively acidic soils it is believed that orthophosphate ions are precipitated or sorbed by species of Al (III) and Fe(III). In alkaline soils orthophosphate may react with calcium carbonate to form relatively insoluble hydroxylapatite :

$$6HPO_4^{2-} + 10CaCO_3 + 4H_2O \rightarrow Ca_{10}(PO_4)_6(OH_2)\downarrow + 10HCO_3^- + 2OH^- \qquad (5.2)$$

In general, because of these reactions little phosphorus applied as fertilizer leaches from the soil. This is important from the standpoint of both water pollution and utilization of phosphate fertilizers.

5.9 Organic Matter in Soil

Although a good soil may behaving less than 5% organic matter, the organic matter in soil plays a vital important role in determining soil productivity. It serves as a source of food for microorganisms in soil, undergoes chemical reactions such as cation exchange reactions, and helps to determine the physical properties of the soil. Among the biologically active components of the organic fraction of soil have been polysaccharides, amino sugars, nucleotides, and organic sulfur and phosphorus compounds. Most of the organic matter in soil consists of a water-insoluble, relatively nonbiodegradable material called humus. Humus is composed of base-soluble fractions called humic and fulvic acids and an insoluble fraction called humin.

Humic materials constitute the most important class of complexing agents. They show high uptake of heavy polyvalent cations.

One of the primary sources of degradation-resistant organic matter in soil is lignin. Wood and the structural material of woody plants consists of cellulose in combination with lignin, a polymeric substance with a higher carbon content than cellulose. Aromatic groups connected by alkyl chains, methoxyl groups, and hydroxyl groups are among the prominent chemical components of lignin. Lignin serves as a "cement" to hold plant material together.

The accumulation of organic matter in soil is strongly influenced by temperature and the availability of oxygen.

Humic materials in soil strongly sorb many solutes in soil water. They have a particular affinity for heavy polyvalent cations. Soil humic substances may contain levels of uranium more than 10^4 that of water with which they are in equilibrium. Thus waters become depleted of their cations (or purified) in passing through humic-rich soils. Humic substances in soils also have a strong affinity for organic compounds such as DDT or Atrazine, a herbicide widely used to kill weeds in corn fields.

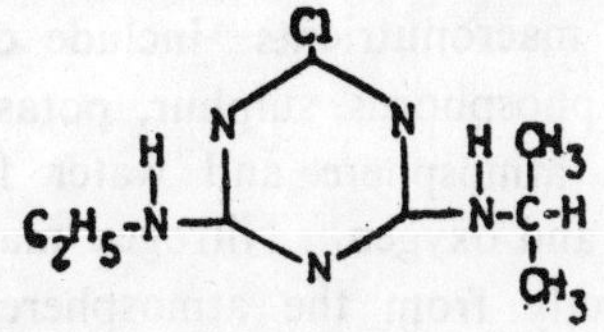

In some cases there occurs strong interaction between the organic and inorganic portions of soil. This is especially true of the strong complexes formed between clays and humic (fulvic) acid compounds. In many soils 50-100% of soil carbon is complexed with clay. These complexes play a role in determining the physical properties of soil, soil fertility, and stabilization of soil organic matter.

Both mineral and organic fractions of soils exchange cations. Humus shows very high cation exchange capacity (300-400 meq/100 g). The cations in soil are leached by carbonic acid in the soil and exchanged for H^+.

$$\text{(Soil) } Ca^{2+} + 2CO_2 + 2H_2O \rightarrow \text{(Soil) } H^+ + Ca^{2+} \text{ (root)} + 2HCO_3^- \quad (5.1)$$

Thus, essential trace-level metals are made available to plants as nutrients.

In the mineral portion of soil, the metal-oxide surface develops negative charge at high pH and exchanges for anions :

$$-\overset{\overset{\displaystyle O}{|}}{M} - OH^- + HPO_4^{2-} \rightleftharpoons -\overset{\overset{\displaystyle O}{|}}{M} - OPO_3H^{2-} + OH^-$$

5.10 Macro-Nutrients in Soil

Plant nutrients may be grouped into macronutrients and micronutrients. Macronutrients are those elements which occur insubstantial levels in plant materials of fluids in the plant. Micronutrients are elements which are essential only at very low levels and generally are required for the function of essential enzymes.

The essential macronutrients include carbon, hydrogen, oxygen, nitrogen, phosphorus, sulphur, potassium, calcium and magnesium. The atmosphere and water form the sources of carbon, hydrogen and oxygen. Nitrogen may be obtained by some plants, directly from the atmosphere, through nitrogen fixing bacteria. The other essential macronutrients are obtained from the soil. Nitrogen, phosphorus and potassium (NPK) are usually added to soil as fertilizers.

Calcium deficiency in soil occurs due to calcium uptake by plants, leaching by carbonic acid in acid soils, and competition with high levels of sodium, potassium and magnesium in alkaline soils. Calcium-deficient soils are usually treated with lime (liming) to provide the necessary calcium supply for plants.

Magnesium has been made available to plants through ion-exchanging organic matter or clays which hold magnesium rather strongly, Magnesium-deficiency in soil has been attributed to the high levels of calcium, sodium or potassium.

Sulfur is assimilated by plants as the sulfate ion, SO_4^{2-}. In addition, in areas where the atmosphere in contaminated with SO_2, sulfur may be absorbed as sulfur dioxide by plant leaves.

Soils deficient in sulfur do not support plant growth well, largely because sulfur is a component of some essential amino acids and of thiamin and biotin. Sulfate ion is generally present in the soils as immobilized insoluble sulfate minerals or as soluble salts which are readily leached from the soil and lost as soil water runoff. Unlike the case of nutrient cations such as K^+, little sulfate is adsorbed to the soil (that is, bound by ion exchange binding) where it is resistant to leaching while still available for assimilation by plant roots.

The reaction of FeS_2 with acid in acid-sulfate soils may release H_2S which is very toxic to plants, and which also kills many beneficial microorganisms. Toxic hydrogen sulfide can also be produced by reduction of sulfate ion through micro-organism-mediated reactions with organic matter.

$$SO_4^{2-} + 2CH_2O + 2H^+ = H_2S + 2CO_2 + 2H_2O \quad (5.1)$$

Production of hydrogen sulfide in flooded soils may be inhibited by treatment with oxidizing compounds, one of the most effective of which is KNO_3.

5.11 Micro-Nutrients in Soil

For plants, the essential micronutrients have been boron, chlorine, sodium, copper, iron, manganese, zinc, vanadium and molybdenum. These elements are needed at trace levels and, if present at higher levels, have a toxic effect. Most of these act as components of essential enzymes. Some of them, such as chlorine, manganese, iron, zinc and vanadium may be involved in photosynthesis.

5.12 Pollution of Soil

The addition of materials to soils by man, arises from the use of agriculture chemicals such as herbicides, fungicides and insecticides, from dustfail and precipitation and use of fertilizers and contaminated water. Whether the material becomes a problem or not, depends on the soil type and the levels. In many situations the problems occur later, when the elements are leached into waterways. Chemical fertilizers are a source of trace metals, either added deliberately, or as an impurity. For example, Cd, As and Pb, common trace metals in rock phosphate, are also in superphosphate. This source of trace metals may not be a problem yet, but this may change as more are added, with increased use of fertilizers.

Serious cadmium pollution of soil occurred in Japan. Over a 20 year period around 100 people (mostly older women) living near the Jintsu River died of a syndrome called Itai-Itai (Ouch-Ouch) disease. The effects were severe and painful bone damage. Bones were easily fractured and twisted, and the effects took around 5-10 years and in some cases up to 30 years, to manifest themselves. In 1962, cadmium was found to be the cause, the source was traced to a zinc mine (Cd is closely associated with

Zn ores) 50 km upriver. The water from the river was used by the people to irrigate the rice paddy fields. The Cd now in the soil, in a number of places >3.0 ppm, was taken up by the rice plants and consumed by the people. Studies in the area demonstrated a close correlation between levels of Cd in the soil and the percentage of women over 50 years with the disease. Mean cadmium levels in rice of 0.68 μg^{-1} (wet weight) was ten times greater than from other areas of Japan. Cadmium water levels were found to be 1 $\mu g\ l^{-1}$ in well water, 5-61 $\mu g\ l^{-1}$ (mean 17 $\mu g\ l^{-1}$) in mine waste water and 1-9 $\mu g\ l^{-1}$ in the river. A possible reason why older women were mainly affected was that they also suffered from a deficiency of vitamin D (from a lack of sunshine). This, together with the high cadmium intake, gave rise to the very painful and often fatal disease. This situation highlights the complexity of the interrelation of more than one contributing factor.

5.13 Wastes and Pollutants in Soil

Soil gets large quantities of waste products each year. Much of the sulfur dioxide evolved in the burning of sulfur-containing fuels ends up on soil as sulfates. Atmospheric nitrogen oxides get converted to nitrates in the atmosphere, and the nitrates eventually are deposited on soil. Soil sorbs NO and NO_2 readily, and these gases get oxidized to nitrate in the soil. Carbon monoxide gets converted to CO_2 and possibly biomass by soil bacteria and fungi. Particulate lead from automobile exhausts is found at elevated levels in soil along heavily traveled highways. Lead from lead mines and smelters occurs at elevated levels on soil near such facilities.

Soil gets enormous quantities of pesticides as an inevitable result of their application to crops. The degradation and eventual fate of these pesticides on soil largely determines the ultimate environmental effects of the pesticides, and detailed knowledge of this is now needed for licensing of a new pesticide. Among the factors to be considered are the sorption of the pesticide by soil, leaching of the pesticide into water as related to its potential for water pollution, effects of the pesticide on microorganisms and animal life in the soil, and possible production of relatively more toxic degradation produsts. Fortunately soil is considered to be an efficient waste disposal system if it is not overloaded. It generally absorbs pesticides well and minimizes their effects on many organisms. In addition soil acts as a good supporting medium for microbial and chemical activities which degrade pesticides.

The three primary ways in which pesticides are degraded in, or on, soil include biodegradation, chemical degradation, or photochemical reactions. Various combinations of these may operate in the degradation of a pesticide.

Although insects, earthworms, and plants may play important roles in the biodegradation of pesticides, microorganisms have been the most important.

Chemical degradation of pesticides has been observed experimentally is soils and clays sterilized to remove all microbial activity. For example, clays have been shown to catalyze the hydrolysis of 0,0-Dimethyl 0-2, 4, 5-trichlorophenyl thiophosphate (also called Trolene, ronnel, etrolene, or trichlorometafos) an effect which is attributed to – OH groups on the mineral surface. Many other purely chemical hydrolytic reactions of pesticides take place in soil.

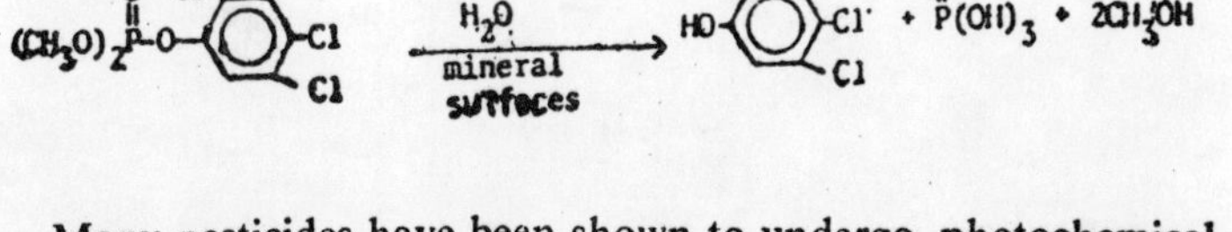

Many pesticides have been shown to undergo photochemical reactions, that is, chemical reactions brought about by the absorption of light. Frequently isomers of the pesticides are produced as products. Many of the studies reported apply to pesticides in water or on thin films, and the photochemical reactions of pesticides on soil and plant surfaces remain largely a matter of speculation. An interesting possibility has been that some soil molecules can get excited by the absorption of light and subsequently react with pesticide molecules to produce additional degradation.

Pesticide residues on crops and food products bring about long-term health hazards.

It may be concluded that the quality of soil is having an impact on public health standards through the human food chain. The environmental health aspects of soil deserve serious attention in the near future.

6

Introduction to Environmental Impact Assessment

Introduction

Concern for environmental quality is a recent phenomenon. The two major criteria, *i.e.*, the project should maximise economic return, and it should be technically feasible, are no longer considered adequate to decide the desirability or even the viability of the project. It is now widely recognized that the development effort frequently produces not only sought for benefits, but other-often unanticipated undesirable consequences as well which may nullify the socio-economic benefits for which the project is designed. The objective of environmental impact assessment is to achieve sustained development with (a) minimal environmental degradation, and (b) prevention of long term environmental adverse effects by incorporating suitable mitigative measures. Environmental impact assessment process, therefore, involves evaluation of environmental implications and incorporation of necessary safeguards for those activities having a bearing on environmental quality. Evaluation of the beneficial and adverse effects of development projects, on the eco-system is attempted, both qualitatively as well as quantitatively.

Impact assessment is a concept that evolved in the search for ways to render development and protection of the environment compatible in the complex and interdependent world of today.

The speed, scale and character of contemporary technological and economic development, which has permitted material standards of living to reach high levels has also led to unforeseen effects on the very environmental assets that constitute the basis for sustained socio-economic development. It is becoming clear that air, water and soil must, of necessity be treated as precious natural resources requiring careful management. Simple cures for pollution problems are no longer sufficient. Comprehensive policies for preventive action to avert environmental damage before it occurs are becoming imperative. In this context, the wide application of procedures for the assessment of environmental impact has become a promising instrument to prepare for public decision-making on development action.

To be really meaningful impact assessment has to be taken up at the project inception stage so that the selection of site, choice of process technology, selection of appropriate layout and building material can be done to ensure environmental compatibility. Making environmental parameters an integral part of the project also ensures that necessary safeguards, monitoring mechanism required for feed-back and mid-course corrections, if any, both in the short and long term can be planned not just for the individual project but for the eco-system as a whole by fully utilising the concept of "carrying capacity" of the system which essentially consists of air, water, soil flora and fauna. The social component which remains sadly neglected and often adversely affects the proper sections of the society whenever rehabilitation is involved, also needs to be incorporated to ensure that quality of life for the affected people is improved after the introduction of a development project rather than bringing them more misery. This is specially so where the affected population happens to be predominently tribals or Adivasis.

Environmental appraisal of projects is an important responsibility of the Department of Environment (DoE) Government of India. Accordingly, questionnaires and guidelines have been evolved development projects in selected sectors such as industry, river-valley, hydel, thermal and atomic power, ports and harbours, mining, etc. The questionnaires and guidelines are updated periodically to facilitate relevant data collection necessary for critical analysis of the project from environmental angle. Guidelines for siting of industries have also been brought out.

Presently the DoE have Environmental Appraisal Committees for following sectors of development project/activities :

—Rever valley projects/irrigation hydel power and multi-purpose;

—Mining projects;

—Industrial Projects; and

—Thermal power projects

Speeial expert groups/committees and task forces are constituted for assessment of other major projects referred to the DoE from time to time.

Before going into the intricate details of the Environmental Impact Assessment it will be worthwhile here to briefly discuss the few terms which will be frequently used in the lesson.

Environmental Inventory

Environmental inventory is a complete description of the environment as it exists in an area where a particular proposed action is being considered. The inventory is compiled from a checklist of descriptors for the physical, and cultural environment. The physical environment includes such major areas as geology, topography, surface-water and groundwater resources, water quality, air quality, and climatology. The biological environment refers to the flora and fauna of the area, including species of trees, grasses, fish, herpetofauna, birds and mammals. Specific reference must be made to any rare and/or endangered plant and animal species. General biological features such as species diversity and overall ecosystem stability should also be presented. Items in the cultural environment include human population trends and population distributions, historic and archaeological sites, and economic indicators of human welfare.

The environmental inventory serves as the basis for evaluating the potential impacts on the environment, both beneficial and adverse, of a proposed action. It is included in an impact statement in the section referred to as "description of the existing environment" or "description of the environmental setting without the project". Development of the inventory represents an initial step in the environmental impact assessment process.

Environmental Assessment

The environmental assessment represents the key step in meeting the legal requirements. In essence, it is an attempt to evaluate the consequences of a proposed action on each of the descriptors in the environmental inventory. The essential steps in an environmental impact assessment are

1. Prediction of the anticipated change in an environmental descriptor.
2. Determination of the magnitude or scale of the particular change.
3. Application of an importance or significance factor to the change.

Many of the current assessment approaches embody the steps of prediction, scaling, and significance interpretation, although the methods use many terms to describe these particular steps.

The scientific validity of the technology available for the prediction of impacts varies depending upon the particular environmental descriptor. For example, extensive research and sound scientific methods have been develop. d for prediction of air quality impacts, at least with regard to anticipated concentration levels of pollutants in the ambient air; however, impact in flora or founa as a result of the calculated concentration levels are less quantifiable. Thus, it is possible to utilize sound technology for some impact predictions, whereas other predictions must be primarily based on professional judgment.

In order to accomplish on environmental assessment, as well as to prepare an inventory and write an impact statement, it is necessary that the approach used be interdisciplinary, systematic, and reproducible. Requirements for an interdisciplinary approach indicate that the environment must be considered in its broadest sense; thus the input of persons trained in number of technical fields needed to be included. The disciplines represented a specific environmental assessment must be oriented to the unique features of the proposed action and the environmental setting however, at a minimum it is necessary to have input from a physical scientist or engineer, a biologist, and a person who can address cultural and socioeconomic impacts. Requirements for a systematic and reproducible approach indicate that a degree of organization and uniformity should be utilized in the assessment process. In this regard several assessment methodologies have been developed since 1970, and these will be discussed in more detail later.

Environment Impact Statement

The environmental Impact Statement (EIS) is a document written in the format as specified by DoE. The ESI represents a summary of the environmental inventory and the findings of the environmental assessment.

There are two categories of EISs : draft statements and final statements. The draft statement is the document prepared by an agency proposing an action; it is circulated for review and comment to other federal agencies, state and local agencies, and public and private interest groups. The final statement is the draft statement modified to include a discussion of problems and objections raised by reviewers. The final statement must be on file with DoE for at least a 30-day period prior to initiation of construction on a project.

Participants. The various participants in the EIA process should be clearly identified , Following is a list of those that are normally involved ;

Decision maker	Can be a head of state, a group of ministers, an elected body, or a single designated individual.
Assessor	Is the person, agency, or company having responsibility for preparing the EIS.
Proponent	can be a government agency or a private firmwishing to initiate the project.
Reviewer	is the person, agency or board with responsibility for reviewing the EIS and assuring compliance with published guidelines or regulations.
Other agencies of government	Are agencies with a special interest in the project; they may be associated with provinces, states, cities or villages.
Expert advisors	Are persons with the specialized knowledgerequired to evaluate the proposed action; they may come from within or outside the government service.
Public at large	Includes citizens and the media.
Special-interest groups	Includes environmental organizations, labour unions, professional societies, and local associations.

Historical Perspective

When a new project or development is planned which might affect environmental quality, an environmental impact assessment (EIA) may be carried out. In most jurisdictions, an EIA is mandatory before permission is given to procceds with designated classes of engineering works. This is certainly the case for major developments such as power stations, flood-control systems, and smelters. However, smaller projects may also be included within EIA regulations. A list of development projects that may require an EIA is given in Table 1 on next page.

Table 1

Development Projects that may Require an Environmental Impact Assessment

	Type of Project	*Example*
1.	Land use and transformation	Urban; industrial; agricultural; airport; transportation; transmission lines; off-shore structures.
2.	Resource extraction	Drilling; mining; blasting; lumbering; commercial fishing and hunting.
3.	Resource renewal	Reforestation; wildlife management; fertilization; waste recyling; flood control.
4.	Agricultural processes	Farming; ranching, dairying; feedlots; irrigation.
5.	Industrial processes	Iron and stell mills; petrochemical industry; smelters; pulp and paper plants.
6.	Transportation	Railways; aircraft; automobiles; trucks; shipping; pipe lines.
7.	Energy	Artificial lakes; dams; oil exploration, refining, and transmission; coal and nuclear power stations.
8.	Waste disposal and treatment	Ocean dumping; landfill; environmental contaminants and toxic substances; underground storage; biological emissions.
9.	Chemical treatment	Insect control (insecticides); weed control (herbicides).
10.	Recrction	Hunting areas; parks; resort development; all-terrain vehicles.

As early as the 1950s. EIAs of major developments were undertaken, particularly in North America, Europe, and Japan. The main objective was to ensure that public safety and health were adequately protected. Separate documents were submitted to each of the regulatory agencies involved (*e.g.*, water authority, air pollution control branch, etc.), and no attempt was made to prepare a comprehensive overview. In the case of an EIA for a dam, calculations were undertaken to ensure that the structure could withstand major floods, based on return periods of precipitation and runoff extremes. Similarly, chimneys were designed on the basis of atmospheric diffusion models to ensure that ground-level concentrations of the pollutants would not exceed air quality standards. These analyses were reviewed by the appropriate regulatory bodies, although not by the public. In the case of the nuclear energy industry, detailed field investigations were also required before an operating permit would be authorized.

The environmental movement of the 1960s and early 1970s, pioneered by people such as Rachel Carson, Barbara Ward, and Barry Commoner, resulted in environmental groups becoming politically active in many countries. As a partial response to these pressure groups, governments accepted the principle that citizens' organizations should have an opportunity to participate in the decision-making process of those major developments which could have significant environmental impacts.

In the early 1970s there was a greater environmental awareness, a realization of limited natural resources, a requirement for greater public accountability by government and industry, and an increased desire by the public to become intimately and actively involved in the planning process. The need to overcome deficiencies in project evaluation techniques became apparent and brought about the birth of the environmental impact assessment process.

The first comprehensive environmental legislation in the United States, the National Environmental Policy Act (NEPA), came into force on January 1, 1970. The act contained three main sections :

1. A declaration of national policy, and with it, a prescription of environmental goals which the federal government was to pursue.
2. A specification that federal agencies must prepare EISs on those federal actions significantly affecting the quality of the human environment.
3. The institutionalization of the EIA process in the Executive Office of the President through the establishment of the Council on Environmental Quality.

In Canada, the federal government established an Environmental Assessment and Review Process in 1973 to ensure that :

1. Environmental effects would be taken into account early in the planning of new federal projects, programmes, and activities.
2. An environmental assessment would be carried out before committments or irrevocable decisions were made, for all projects which might have an adverse effect on the environment (projects with potentially significant environmental effects would be submitted to the Department of the Environment for review).
3. The results of the assessments would be used in planning, decision making, and implementation.

The need for carrying out an environmental impact assessment has been accepted in many other jurisdictions, including most U.S. states, Canadian provinces, Japan, Australia, and several European countries.

The EIA process has been evolving since the early 1970s. At that time the emphasis was on measurable physical factors, particularly those for which there were standards and codes (*e.g.*, air quality, water quality, solid waste disposal). After a few years, EIAs began to include biological and ecological factors, even though they were difficult to quantify. More recently, EIAs were broadened event further to include socioeconomic factors (employment opportunities, cultural impacts, recreational factors, etc.), so that trade-offs among socioeconomic and environmental factors could be evaluated. In some juridictions, the EIA process is also being used to evaluate class actions (*e.g.*, to ban a pesticide and to regulate the lead content of gasoline).

The EIA system has been welcomed in principle by many scientists, engineers, citizens' group and others. In practice, however, the process has left much to be desired. For example, EISs are often too long and too technical (for the citizens' groups), and do not deal with the environment in a holistic way. However, a learning process is taking place, which is improving the usefulness of EISs decision-shaping documents.

At present, the environmental impact assessment process is being redefined to integrate biophysical impacts, social and community impacts, as well as technical and economic impacts, into a comprehensive and holistic process which relates human aspirations to biophysical limitations as well as technical and economic realitites. This process permits decision-makers to determine whether certain developments are acceptable, and to avoid or mitigate adverse effects. It also requires that the decision-maker be made more accountable to the public for a particular action.

Environmental Assessment Process

Fig. 6.1 shows five activities in the environmental assessment process. Certain basics, which are required to accomplish an environmental assessment, are related to the description of the environmental setting, impact prediction and assessment, and preparation of the EIS.

In order to be able to predict and assess the impacts associated with a proposed action, it is necessary to describe the environmental setting in which the proposed action is to take place. This gives the baseline information against which prediction and assessment can be made. The description of the environmental setting also provides input information for preparation of the EIS.

The major step in the environmental assessment process, and the step that requires the greatest degree of scientific application of technology, is impact prediction and assessment, this particular step involves projecting the environmental setting into the future without the proposed action and then performing the necessary calculations or studing the approaches for actually predicting the impact of the proposed action and assessing the consequences. Information from this step becomes a part of the next step involving aggregation of information becomes a part of the EIS.

The next step is the aggregation of the impact information on each alternative. Based on this aggregated information, as well as on other decision factors such as technical and economic considerations, the proposed action is selected. Information about this step of the environmental aessessment process also becomes a part of the EIS.

Finally, the last step involves the preparation of a draft EIS in accordance with specified guidelines of DoE. The draft impact statement circulated for review and comment, and following the incorporation of the review comments, a final EIA is prepared and filed with the DoE. Thirty days following the filing, the proposed action may be initiated.

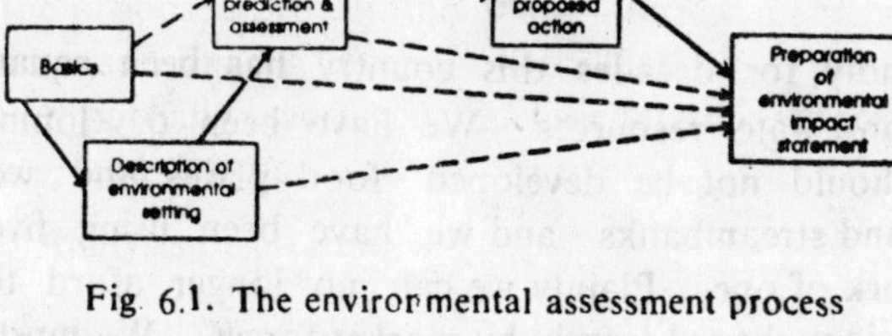

Fig. 6.1. The environmental assessment process

It is realized that this environmental assessment process is idealized and that it assumes the environmental assessment is conducted early in project planning so that environmental considerations can actually become a part of the decision among alternatives for solving a particular problem. Strict adherence to these steps is not absolutely necessary in all cases; however, this does represent an approach that can be used and is generally applicable.

Finally we can say that the first step in the EIA process is to determine whether a project falls within the relevant act or regulations, and whether the development is likely to create significant environmental disruption. If so, an assessment is undertaken, leading to the preparation of an EIS. In some jurisdictions, the EIS is open to public scrutiny and may be reviewed at public hearings. Eventually a decision is made at the political level as to whether to :

1. Accept the development,
2. Accept an amended form of the proposed development,
3. Accept an alternative proposal or
4. Reject the development.

Goals of EIA Process

Environmental goals may fall into three categories : clean up, controlled land use, and social welfare. The first goal is to set straight the mistake of the past cleaning up our air and water, recovering and recycling wastes, and controlling pesticides and toxic substances. Generally, we know what needs to be done. We have much of the necessary technology and we are working to develop that which we do not yet have.

Secondly, for decades this country has been squandering its land and water resources. We have been developing land which should not be developed – food plains and weltands, ravines and streambanks – and we have been using five acres to do work of one. Plainly we can no longer aford to have key decisions shaped largely by market forces. We must move toward some form of land use control.

Thirdly, the rapid physical deterioration of our cities and the critical human problems accompanying this decline pose an enormous challenge to the stability of our nation. To meet this challenge, a much broader mere physical comfort and freedom from want in any material sense. Indeed, the essence of quality urban living lies in its diversity and complexity. As such, achieving a better environment for our cities will involve not only providing for physical needs such as litter-free streets, clean air and water, houses free of rate and lead-based paint, and maintenance of natural surroundings,—but much more. The goal must include adequate health, housing, education, jobs, recreation, cultural opportunities, and means of transportation. It also demands, particularly for the people of our inner cities, a sense of personal dignity, self-respect, community involvement, and participation in decisions which affect their lives.

Increasing demand for environmental quality and cleaner surroundings places a high priority on the quality of natural surroundings as it affects human well being. Protection of scenery, clean air and water, minimization of noise, congestion, and nonotonous city scapes, and open space for active outdoor recreation have all taken on new importance. There is great concern fouman health and a desire to live, work, and play in more pleasant surroundings. For the planner and impact analyst these have proved to be very important considerations.

Basic Contents of an Impact Statement

There are five points that need to be adhered to in an EIS. The first one is to describe "the environmental impact of the proposed action." In the early years of the preparation of impact statements, attention was primarily focused to the negative or detrimental impacts associated with a given proposed action. To be complete both beneficial and detrimental impacts should be delineated.

Later on it was recognized that both the positive and negative ramifications of a given proposed action should be explored in complete detail. In addition, attention must also be directed toward the primary and secondary impacts associated with a proposed action. Primary and secondary impacts also referred to as direct and indirect consequences. In general, agencies have developed methods and procedures to respond in part to direet impacts, both beneficial and adverse. However, the major impact of a project is often from secondary or even tertiary effects, and these are much more difficult to assess due to the dearth of predictive techniques available.

The second item required is an identification of "any adverse environmental effects which cannot be avoided should the proposal be implemented." If a thorough approach has been utilized in describing the environmental impact of the proposed action, this section should basically be an abstract of the negative impacts, both direct and indirect, of the proposed action. New information is not included in this section.

The third point focuses on a discussion of "alternatives to the proposed action." This section has caused a great deal of difficulty, and many court cases have resulted from inadequate treatment of this section by the proposing agency. Implicit in the alternatives section is the idea that the alternatives to the proposed action should be compared on a common basis, presumably their relative or absolute environmental impact. One alternative that should be discussed is the no-action, or no-project, alternative. This alternative requires the proposing agency to predict what the future environment will be without the project, and it serves as the basis against which impacts of the proposed action can be compared. One point to be considered in the alternative section is an evaluation of the alternatives through a public participation program.

The fourth item is a description of "the relationship between local short-term uses of man's environment and the maintenance and enhancement of long-term productivity." This section is based on the principle that each generation should serve as trustee of the environment for succeeding generations; therefore, attention must be paid to the question of whether options for future use of the environment are being eliminated by the particular proposed action. In a pragamatic sense many impact statements have described the impacts associated with the construction phase to be short-term and the operational phase to be long term.

The last point is a discussion of "any irreversible and irretrievable commitments of resources which would be involved in the proposed action should it be implemented." Semantic difficulties are encountered with the terms irreversible and irretrievable. Again from a practical standpoint, most impact statements focus attention on possible changes on land usage as a result of a proposed action, loss of cultural features such as archaeological or historical sites, preclusion of development of underground mineral resources, loss of habitat for plants and animals, loss of impact on rare and endangered plants and/or animals, material required for project construction, energy usage required during project utilization, and even the human and monetary expenditures involved.

Basic to the Process

There are several prerequisites that must be fulfilled for a proper environmental assessment to be accomplished. These prerequisites or basic are as follows :

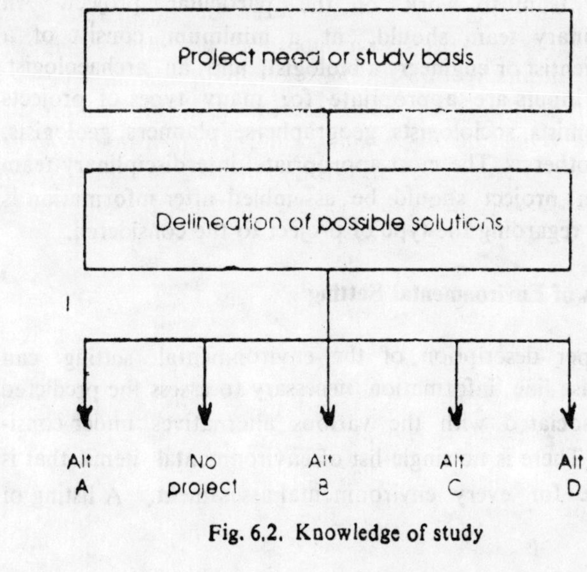

Fig. 6.2. Knowledge of study

Since difference types of projects exert different impacts upon the environment and different alternatives for a given need exert different environmental impacts upon the environment, it is necessary to be familiar with the need for the project and the general types of possible solutions. This concept is shown in Fig. 6.2 After the identification of the need for a project or a study, it is necessary to identify certain possible alternative solutions for meeting the project need, including alternatives that might be outside the legislative responsibility of the proposing agency. Since one of the alternatives that must be considered in a proposed action is the non-project alternative, it is necessary to include that alternative along with other technical and managerial possibilities. Completely knowledge of the types of impacts associated with various alternatives is necessary. For example, alternatives to a multipurpose reservoirs and development of alternative water supplies. The environmental impacts of the construction of a level differ from those associated with the construction of a multipurpose reservoir. Therefore it is necessary to know the types of alternatives that are under consideration.

Based on the general knowledge of project need and possible alternative solutions, it is necessary to asse bly an interdisciplinary team to work on the particular project. An interdisciplinary team should, at a minimum, consist of a physical scientist or engineer, a biologist, and an archaeologist. Additional inputs are appropriate for many types of projects from economists, sociologists, geographers, planners, geologists, and many others. The most appropriate interdisciplinary team for a given project should be assembled after information is aggregated regarding the type of project to the considered.

Description of Environmental Setting

A proper description of the environmental setting can provide base-line information necessary to assess the predicted impacts associated with the various alternatives under consideration. There is no single list of environmental items that is appropriate for every environmental assessment. A listing of environmental items should be developed on a project-by-project basis or at least a project-type-by-type-basis.

One of the best approaches for assembling a list of items is to have knowledge of the types of impacts associated with given types of projects. For example, in the preparation of airport environmental impact statements it is necessary to consider the impact of airport operations both air quality and noise; thus it is required to have a description of the air quality and the noise levels in the vicinity of the proposed airport prior to its development.

Many guidelines contain detailed descriptions of the items to be included in an environmental setting. Guidelines vary as to the detail suggested for these various environmental items. At a minimum it is necessary to cover those subjects specified in the guidelines associated with the agency proposing the action.

Great value can be derived from analyzing the EIS work by others. The approximately 6,000 EISs that have been prepared represent an extensive pool of information, which, if properly analyzed, can be of value in preparing a description of the environmental setting. For example, if the project is to describe the environmental setting associated with a dredging operation, it would be of great value to examine the environmental setting in several dredging impact statements and to develop a master list of items to be included in the statement at hand.

Another approach that can serve as a basis for describing the environmental setting is the listing of environmental items included in several developed methodologies for impact analysis. Many of the methodologies contain from 50 to 100 different environmental items for which impact prediction and assessment is suggested. In order to be able to properly accomplish this assessment, environmental setting information must be accrued for each item in the methodology.

Using the four suggested bases for developing a list of environmental items, it is then desirable to compartmentalize the environment into several areas. One suggested arrangement is to divide the environment into phｙsical-chemical parameters or items, biological parameters, and socioeconomic parameters.

Impact prediction and Assessment

To properly predict and assess the impact of a proposed action, it is first necessary to describe the future environmental setting in the area without the project. Various techniques are available for projecting current conditions into the future based on historical trends. Less quantitative approaches are also available for predicting alternative futures based on management decisi on without the continuance of historical trends.

Prediction and assessment of the impact of each alternative on the physical-chemical, biological, cultural, and socioeconomic environment are required. There are many scientific approaches and models that can be used to predict impacts on the air environment, water environment, and noise environment. Less quantitative, although not entirely subjective, methods are available for predicting the impacts of alternatives on the biological environment, the prediction of impacts on the cultural environment is largely associated with determination of the geographic distribution of cultural resources in the project area. Since this determination requires on-site survey work, this impact prediction is perhaps the most precise one that can be accomplished. However, since many studies do not have the necessary funding for on-site archaeological surveys, if scientific extrapolation has to be made from known history and known sites in the general vicinity, this impact prediction then becomes the least precise area of prediction. Finally, prediction of impacts on the socio-economic environment does have technological bases. However, most of the projections for socioeconomic considerations, such as population and population distribution, are largely based on historical trends.

Assessment of the Consequences of predicted impacts is approached in different ways dipending upon the environmental compartment. For example, predicted changes in air and water quality can be assessed against environmental quality standards, whereas predicted changes in land use and the resultant consequences on floral and faunal species are more difficult to assess.

Most of the methodologies of impact analysis involve the concept of an impact scale and an impact importance. Example of scaling include comparison with established environmental quality standards, use of straight-line interpolations, and use of environmental parameter functions. Professional judgment can also be used in absence of any standards or formalized assessment methodologies. The subjective assignment of significance or importance to each of the environmental items is an important consideration. Perhaps the most-used technique involves considering each item as having nearly equal importance, with focus being given to the major items determined through professional judgment. More formalized approaches have been developed, including ranked pairwise comparison and importance grouping.

Selection of Proposed Action

In an idealized environmental assessment, selection of the proposed action should be accomplished only after consideration of the environmental, technical, and economic factors associated with each alternative for meeting the project. In many instances selection of the proposed action is made prior to the environmental assessment; however, DoE guidelines encourage the selection based on grounds other than technical and economic factors. The first element of this step is aggregation and display of the comparative environmental impacts of each alternative, include the non-project alternative. Various techniques are available for aggregating the information, including the multiplication of scaling and importance values in some techniques and the use of professional judgment in others.

In addition to the relative environmental impacts associated with alternatives, information should also be displayed on other decision factors for each alternative, including unique technical considerations or technical difficulties associates with an alternative; economic analyses, perhaps based on the benefit cost ratio or excess benefits minus costs; and general public preference for an alternative if public meetings have been held in conjunction with the proposed action

The selection of the alternative to become the proposed action for the project can be based on professional judgment or on some decision-making technique such as the use of weighted rankings.

Preparation of Environmental Impacts Statement

The last step in the environmental assessment process involves the preparation of a draft EIS, the subjection of this draft statement to review and comment by others, and the preparation of a final EIS and subsequent filing of this final statement with the DoE. The general sequence of events in this step is as follows :

Prepare draft EIS

1. Description of proposed action, project purposes, and environmental setting.
2. Relationship of the proposed action to land-use plans, policies, and controls for the affected area.
3. Probable impact of the proposed action on the environment.
4. Alternatives to the proposed action.
5. Any probable adverse environmental effects that cannot be avoided.
6. Relationship between local short-term uses of the human environment and the maintenance and enhancement of long-term productivity.
7. Any irreversible and irretrievable commitments of resources that would be involved in the proposed action should it be implemented.

8. An indication of what other interests and considerations are thought to offset the adverse environ mental effects of the proposed action.

Circulate draft EIS to others for review and comment

1. Federal agencies
2. State and local agencies
3. Public and private interest groups

Prepare final EIS

1. Discuss and incorporate review comments of others
2. File with DoE

The draft EIS should include either separate or combined sections that address each of the eight points shown above. Following preparation of a draft EIS and its internal review by an agency, it should be circulated to others for review and comment. The reviewers should include federal agencies as specified by DoE guidelines, state and local agencies where the proposed action is to occur, and relevant local public and private interest groups.

Review comments from these groups should be incorporated into the draft EIS, and a separate section should be written on these review comments and other public participation associated with the proposed action. Then the final EIS should be filed with the DoE, a filing period of at least 30 days is required prior to initiation of the proposed action.

Though various elements of an EIS have already been introduced, here, a detailed description of each element is presented to give the reader an idea of the various factors that are to be considered for each element of EIS.

1. Project Description

a. "Purpose of the project"

   1. to increase or to provide facility for user group

2. to make use of special techniques to create a worthwhile living environment
3. to provide increased tax base and economic development.
4. to increase employment opportunities
5. to remove substandard structures
6. to rationalize land use patterns

b. "Description of action"

1. Name of project : urban renewal, new structure, etc.
2. Summary of activities :
   (1) estimated total program expenditure
   (2) proportion of expenditure shared by sponsors
   (3) land area
   (4) acquisition of business and housing units, etc.
   (5) residents of the project area and population change
   (6) existing and modified land use
   (7) proposed mixture of structures, architectural programs
   (8) site improvements : streets, sidewalks, street lighting, water, sewer, storm drainage, landscaping and parking
   (9) construction method
   (10) project timing schedule
      a. acquisition phase
      b. construction phase
      c. operational phase
         (1) initial occupancy
         (2) full-scale occupancy
         (3) fluctuations in occupancy
         (4) changes in use

d. close-out phase (restoration or reuse of site)

c. "Environmental setting"

1. Project location

a. boundary : include abbreviated maps to show distance to surrounding facilities, physical characteristics of existing facilities, references to natural boundaries, immediate and regional.

b. location of nearby facilities : airports, highways, parks, central business district, wilderness and wildlife area

2. Environment prior to proposed action

a. Physical character of the area

(1) size : acreage, existing facilities, heights of buildings

(2) landscape : trees, age of trees, types and sizes of trees

(3) existing situation

(4) existing zoning and land use

(5) topography

(6) ecology and soil

(7) seismicity

(8) existing utilities : gas, electricity, water, solid waste, waste water treatment

(9) current public safety : police and fire

(10) parking facilities

(11) transportation facilities

(a) nature of traffic : stop and go

(b) major streets

(c) public transportation : transit, bus, taxi, airport, bus station, train station, etc.

b. Social and economic characteristics of the area

(1) census traits describing the area : income, ethnic, school, welfare, duration of residency, social mix

(2) employment setting

(3) property tax and property ownership

(4) retail activities : supermarket, grocery store, drug store, laundries, banks department stores, beauty parlour, barber shop and corner stores

(5) relocation arrangement : payment and assistance

(6) educational facilities : preschool, elementary, high school, library.

(7) cultural facilities : historical structures, churches, museums, and theaters.

(8) recreational facilities : bars, poolrooms, bowling. etc.

(9) social services ; agencies, societies, groups, welfare departments, missionaries, hospitals.

C. Aesthetic description of area.

(1) Scenic view : mountains, creeks, urban landscape.

(2) Historic sites.

3. Other related Federal activities.

Views of local groups, local officials and citizen's groups, state and Federal agencies concerning the proposed project and other related projects.

Land-use Relationships

Here, the description relates the proposed action to land-use plans, policies and controls for the affected area.

(a) Federal, state, or local policies or standards which are in danger of being violated or ignored.

(b) Relationship to local/area-wide/state planing.

3. Probable Impact of the Proposed Action on the Environment

Discussion must cover both the impact of the proposed project on the environment and the impact of the environment on the project. If should cover :

(1) What will be impacted

(2) Sources of impact

(3) Significance of impact (magnitude and importance)

(a) "Positive and negative effects".

Describe both beneficial and determental aspects of the environmental changes caused by the proposed action.

The following is a set of sample questions that should be asked for a proposed land development Impacts on the Natural Environment :

(1) Is the development controversial ?

(2) Will the development substantially alter the patterns of behaviour for mammals ?

(3) Will the development substantially alter the breeding, nesting, or feeding grounds for birds ?

(4) Will the development substantially alter the patterns of behaviour for fish ?

(5) Will the development substantially alter the behaviour of amphibians or reptiles ?

(6) Will the development substantially alter the patterns of behaviour of insects ?

(7) Will the development cause or increase water pollution ?

(8) Will the development adversely affect the water table in the area ?

(9) Will the development cause or increase air pollution ?

(10) Will the development increase the stability or instability of the soils and/or geology of the site ?

(11) Are the geologic or soil conditions of the site hazardous to continued on-site or off-site human occupance ?

(12) Will the development increase the erosion potential of the site ?

(13) Will the development increase the potential fire hazards of the site ?

(14) Will the development disturb existing vegetation ?

Impacts on the Cultural Environment :

(1) Will the development produce abnormal amounts of traffic ?

(2) Will the development have significant aesthetic effects ?

(3) Will the development divide or disrupt existing land uses (including economic base) ?

( ) Will the development eliminate or deter existing recreational uses ?

(5) Will the development affect areas of unique interest or beauty (including archeological and/or anthropological interest) ?

(b) "Direct and Indirect consequences."

Both primary and secondary significant consequences to the environment should be included in the analysis.

Primary effects. Include direct impacts on man's health and welfare and on other forms of life and related ecosystems. Examples or direct effect might include noise from aircraff operations or benefits from installation of wet scrubbers to meet air quality standards.

Secondary effects. Include secondary and indirect environmental impacts, particularly on population concentration and growth. Many federal actions attract people to previously unpopulated areas, and indirectly cause pollution, congestion, and land development that probably would not have existed otherwise, conversely, other actions may result in displacing population. As an example, noise from aircraft operations may affect future land use patterns in the area, and the results of air pollution abatement operations may produce a secondary water pollution problem from the scrubber waste.

4. Alternatives to the Proposed Action

(a) "Reasonable alternative actions."

Any alternative which is currently technologically practicable or likely to become so within the time frame of the project should be included.

The standard that "all reasonably available alternatives", must be included implies that some reasons for excluding, potential alternatives are not legitimate. Most important, if is irrevalent whether a practicable alternative is or is not within the agency's authority must be included and discussed just as thoroughly as those within. The purpose is to find more environmentally acceptable solutions to problems here so that they may be implemented by whatever means may be necessary.

First, an alternative need only partly achieve the objectives of the proposal; alternatives such as postponenment, scaling down, and no project are in this category. Second, the project objectives may not be so narrowly stated as to rule out attractive alternative supplying roughly similar benefits.

Thus, discuss the full array of alternatives (including no action and those actions beyond the lead agency's immediate control) which would significantly alter the environmental impacts of the proposed project, including alternatives which would reduce adverse impacts, even though other objectives would be affected or partially sacrificed. Include alternative locations or sites, sizes, and designs:

(b) "Analysis of alternatives".

Sufficient analysis of such alternatives, their costs, and impact on the environment should accompany the proposed action through the agency review process in order not to prematurely foreclose options which might have less detrimental effects.

Compare and evaluate the costs and benefits of these alternatives with those of the proposed project, and discuss why they were rejected.

5. Probable Adverse Environmental Effects which Cannot be Avoided

(a) "Adverse and unavoidable impacts"

Discuss the seriousness of the adverse impacts resulting from the recommended action. Describe why the action is being proposed in spite of adverse impact (countervailing interests), and show how environmental aspects have been balanced against technical and financial considerations of the project's anticipated accomplishments.

Such impacts may include the following :

* Water or air pollution resulting from the action;
* Destruction of historical or archaeological sites;
* Disruption of wildlife habitats;
* Increase in urban congestion;
* Threats to heath;
* Undesirable land use patterns.

(b) "How avoidable adverse impacts will be mitigated".

Describe what has been done to minimize adverse impacts which :

(a) Could have been avoided were one of the alternatives adopted;

(b) Could not be avoided by any alternative; and

(c) Were avoided by choosing the recommended action. Discuss the costs of abatement measures, including those rejected. Describe any modifications to the project or provisions added which are designed to enhance environmental quality to eliminate or reduce potential adverse impacts.

For example, the following mitigation statements might be applicable :

*Wildlife and vegetation will be protected by limiting vehicular traffic related to construction activities to those areas which will be disrupted by permanent construction.

*Advance coordination with local public school officials will allow for sufficient planning to accommodate anticipated increased enrollment pressures on local public schools.

*Land areas will be sodded after completion of site clearing, to prevent unnece sary erosion.

*Haul roads will be treated with palliatives to minimize dust production.

Include a discussion of how the lead agency will assure that such provisions will be implemented if the project is approved, *e.g.*, requirements in the contact, grant, or other documents.

6. Relationship between local short-term uses of man's environment and the maintenance and enhancement of long-term productivity

Assess the action for cumulative and long-term effects from the perspective that each generation is trustee of the environment for succeeding generations. Evaluate short-term and long-term environmental and technical/economic costs and benefis. Discuss any future options foreclosed as a result of the recommended action and alternatives which avoid the foreclosure, identify those who benefit and those who pay the costs over time.

7. rreversible and irretrievable commitments of resources which would be involved

Discuss implications to population distribution and land-use and development trends, investment of resources such as land, labour, and community services, and destruction or irreplaceable or unique resources such as historic property and unique natural areas. Identify the extent to which the action curtails the range of beneficial uses of the environment, including options for use of the site or area which are foreclosed. Include primary and secondary impacts. Care should be taken in this section not to merely repeat impacts discussed in previous sections. The focus here is on resource utilization rather than just on the environment.

8. Other interests and considerations of federal policy that offset the adverse environmental effects of the proposed action

After circulation to other agencies for comment, show how substantive comments and recommendations of the other federal, state and local agencies and private parties have been incorporated into the project plans and the Environmental Impact Statement if the Statement has been changed in response to a comment, reference to the page number of the revision may be sufficient). Also explain why recommendations have been rejected. Annex comments received as appropriate.

In the case of some governments, environmental impact assessment is required only for government developments. Projects initiated by the provate sector are excluded. In other jurisdictions, environmental impact assessment is required for specified development, activities and in some cases, all major developments. Even though there does not appear to be a universal rule of application, the some cases, all major development, nature of the development its size and scale of impact, its potential hazard, and its public sensitivity are major factors in determining whether an environmental impact assessment is required.

The procedures used in the review of assessments and the level at which decisions are taken on major developments vary among governments. In some instances, separate and independent review panels are created; in other, interdisciplinary review are undertaken throughout the government. In most cases, elected officials determine whether a development should proceed, and appointed officials determine the necessary terms and conditions. The terms and conditions are usually stipulated in various approvals, permits, or licences and it is left to regulatory agencies to determine satisfactory compliance.

Environmental impacts assessment is seen by many government as part of the planning process for large-scale development projects. The process integrates initial feasibility studies, design, and after implementation. It is seen as a viable tool in achieving a balance between industrial development and maintenance of environmental quality.

There is a trend towards greater standardization of environmental impact assessment by means of legislation, regulations and guidelines. It is hoped that a loss of flexibility through standardization will not result, and that environmental impact assessment procedures will continue to protect the legitimate concerns of the public.

Conclusion

The main objective of an EIS is the reconciliation of environmental and socioeconomic considerations with respect to development and other proposed actions. Accordingly, the EIA system is a potentially useful component of good environmental; management however, as currently practiced, it is far from perfect.

The future of environmental impact assessment will be characterized by manifold activities. More federal guidelines and the passage of additional state and local environmental policy acts will result in the preparation of more EISs. Although more statements will be prepared, it is anticipated that their average length will be reduced because of developing technologies for impact prediction and assessment and methodologies for evaluation of alternatives. Public participation in all phases on environmental decision making will increasingly occur in the future. Finally, current and future research efforts will provide information relevant to many of today's unanswered questions.

